PLAYING FOR MORE

CASE KEENUM

with ANDREW PERLOFF

PLAYING FOR MORE

Trust Beyond
What You
Can See

B&H
PUBLISHING GROUP

NASHVILLE, TENNESSEE

For everyone who ever believed in me

Acknowledgments

It's amazing to sit here and look back at what God has done in my life. Thinking about the first thirty years of my life, and the twists and turns that have brought me here, is incredible. To see it come out on paper has been so rewarding. I really can't believe that this book has come together so quickly. It's been an amazing experience.

I remember sitting at dinner in Minneapolis in February with my wife Kimberly, marketing agent Dusty Stanfield, and friend Andrew Perloff. At some point during dinner it came up that we should write a book. I remember laughing at the notion and saying it sounded like a great dream one day but not thinking much more about it. Now I'm sitting here writing acknowledgments. Crazy.

I really can't thank those people who were at that dinner enough. Dusty has helped orchestrate this thing from the beginning. I can't thank you enough for your friendship and support throughout my career. Jeff, Graylan, and everyone at SSG, thanks for always believing in me and being a voice of reason through all the ups and downs of life in the NFL. Andrew, I know for a fact this would not have happened with any other writer. It has been a true privilege to work on this together and get to know each other so much better in the process. You are very talented and it has been so much fun going through this with you.

The best thing in my life is Christ. After Him, I have no idea where I would be without you, Kimberly. You are my favorite person in the whole world. You've supported, encouraged, and challenged me our entire relationship, and I know I would not be the man I am today if it were not for you. It has been so much fun living life with you and now we wrote a book together!

To my publishers at LifeWay, and literary agent Esther Feddorkevich, y'all are seriously all-stars. From the second we all sat down together, I could tell it was a great fit.

I honestly have so many people to thank. My family has been my rock. Dad, I notice I'm becoming more and more like you every day, whether I like it or not. Thank you for showing me what a real man is. Mom, you are the sweetest, hardest-working person I know. I am a momma's boy at heart and there is not a day that goes by that I don't feel loved and encouraged by you. Lauren and Allison, my wonderful sisters, thank you for putting up with my shenanigans and loving me regardless of this crazy journey. Can't wait to see what life has in store for y'all. Lauren and Justin, I really can't thank you enough for helping me with the book. You're so gifted in so many ways! To my in-laws, the Caddells, you guys have been awesome to me from day one. To our entire family, I love you and thank you for all your support and love through so many ups and downs.

For every coach I've ever had, thank you. Each and every one of you has been like a father to me. I have learned so much from you and will carry it with me for all of my life. You believed in me and instilled confidence in me and kept me going when things got tough.

To all my teammates, past and present, it has been an honor to sweat, bleed, and fight alongside each of you. Football is the best game there is, and the bonds we form playing this great game last a lifetime.

So many people have poured into my life—it's emotional just thinking about them all. All my pastors and chaplains, thanks for being my spiritual leaders.

Mikado, my guy, thanks for always being at my side. Your friendship means the world to me.

Jon and Tracy Sullivan, thank you for opening your home and your hearts to us when we needed it so much and teaching us what a disciple really is!

To all my friends and everyone who has shared this life with us, thank you for your love and support.

Contents

Foreword

I met Case Keenum for the first time in 2011, when he was a senior in college. I had heard about this great young quarterback who was setting all kinds of records at the University of Houston but I hadn't really gotten a chance to see him play. So I was anxious to spend some time with him and get to know him. It didn't take me long to come to the conclusion that he was the type of person you wanted to lead your football team. He had the sort of outgoing personality that made him easy to talk to, and it was combined with a quiet confidence that people rally around. In fact, my short conversation with Case reminded me of one I'd had a decade earlier with a college quarterback named Drew Brees. After visiting with Case for ten minutes I just knew he was a natural leader and I felt that he would have the same type of success in the National Football League that Drew has enjoyed.

Six years later my eleven-year-old son, Justin, got the chance to meet Case during the week leading up to Super

Bowl LII in Minneapolis. Case's Minnesota Vikings had come up short in the NFC Championship Game against the Philadelphia Eagles, but he had led them on a magical season, including a miraculous last-second playoff win over the New Orleans Saints. Justin's first impression of Case was the same as mine had been. He could tell right away there was something uncommon about Case.

That's the vibe that most people get when they spend any time with Case Keenum. It's hard to describe, but he definitely has the "It Factor" that you look for in a quarterback, or in any leader for that matter. It's the ability to help other people be better. The ability to rally people around you and have them believe that somehow you will lead them to great things. They feel that if they stay with you and continue to believe, you can lead them to victory, even in the toughest of circumstances.

That's the feeling you get when you're around Case for any length of time. He's been a leader and a winner all his life and he's demonstrated those qualities since he was a young athlete. And he's done it that not just during the record-breaking performances and the championship seasons, but in the disappointing times as well. He kept the same upbeat attitude when he wasn't highly recruited coming out of high school and when he got injured. When he wasn't drafted coming out of college, he didn't get down but just became more determined to prove the experts wrong. He signed a contract with his hometown Houston Texans but didn't experience the immediate success that he had in college. The first two years of his NFL career provided nothing but disappointments. Through it all, though, he never lost his desire or his belief in his abilities.

Where does that type of attitude come from? In *Playing for More* you'll learn that attitude came from many sources. It came from a very supportive family and a dad who taught him not only how to play quarterback but how to work hard and sacrifice to be the best he could be. It came from some excellent coaches who helped him develop as a player. But, more than anything, I believe you'll see that the driving force in Case Keenum's life is his relationship with Jesus Christ.

As I've gotten to know Case better, I've learned that his primary motivation as a player, and as a leader, is to point people to the Lord. He loves playing the game of football, loves being around his teammates, and he definitively wants to use his gifts to help his team win. But none of those things are the real reason he plays football and why he competes so hard. More than anything else, he wants to show young people that the most important thing in his life is his relationship with Jesus. That's why he plays. That's why he trains so hard and has sacrificed so much to become an excellent player. And that's why he has written this book.

As you read this book you'll get an idea of the hard work and extreme dedication it takes to become an NFL quarterback. You'll learn about the amazing highs and lows in the life of a professional athlete. You'll see some of the traits that have made Case a great husband, a great teammate, and a great friend. But more than anything, I think you'll see what has really motivated Case and made him such an uncommon person, and that's his love of the Lord. And I know that's what he really wants you to get from reading this book.

—Tony Dungy

Prologue

It had to be Drew Brees. *Drew freakin' Brees*—of all the quarterbacks I could possibly face in my first playoff start. A playoff start that at the beginning of the season seemed unlikely since I was the third QB on the depth chart for the Minnesota Vikings. And yet here we were, coming off a remarkable 13–3 season in which I had just put up the best numbers of my NFL career. I had a chance to help bring the Vikings to the NFC conference title game for the first time since 2009 . . . when, coincidentally, Drew Brees and the New Orleans Saints beat the Vikings on the way to his first and only Super Bowl win. I was thinking I would finally win the big game, finally come through for my team when it mattered most, the playoffs. I was living the dream I had played out in my backyard ever since I was a kid.

First, let's set the table: We were down 21–20 to the Saints in a divisional-round playoff game following the 2017 season, and there were three minutes left. I had the ball in my hands with the game on the line. I knew this was it, now-or-never. My teammates stepped up in a big way. My big tight end, Kyle Rudolph, had made contested catch after contested catch all year, and he made his biggest of all on this drive. Running back Jerick McKinnon ripped off two great runs for first downs. And Adam Thielen, one of the best receivers I've ever played with, made a catch I couldn't believe. On a scramble drill he turned his slant route back up the field. I lofted a prayer toward the sideline and he jumped up to make the catch with Pro Bowl cornerback Marshon Lattimore draped all over him. The officials called holding and pass interference on the same play, and somehow it didn't matter. Adam hung on to the ball. Up to that point, it was the biggest moment of our season. *Clutch.* That was one of the most memorable drives of my career. We got into field goal range and Kai Forbath drilled a 53-yarder to give us a 23–21 lead.

I went back to the sideline absolutely pumped. My emotions were soaring. Then I looked at the clock.

One minute and 30 seconds left.

Crap.

Drew Brees.

Our defense was one of the best in the NFL. Heck, it was the best. And all we needed was one stop. But then Brees—a quarterback I've looked up to my whole life, a fellow Texan— took the field. I watch his tape every offseason. I've read his book. I even stole his pregame chant and did it with my boys at the University of Houston. Now Brees was driving, and it was time to start doing the math.

The Saints convert a fourth-and-10 from our 46-yard line—40 seconds left. *If they get a first down, can they run out the clock?* Brees completes a short pass—36 seconds left. *Will I get another chance?* Another completion—33 seconds left. We call a time-out. I can't look anymore. If they convert on third-and-one, game over. Somehow, as hot as Brees and the Saints are, we stop them. They have to settle for a field goal. We're down 24–23 with 25 seconds left. It's not over.

I'd like to say I rallied my teammates on the sideline, maybe gave an inspiring speech like they do in the movies. Cue up Denzel Washington in *Remember the Titans*. "Fake 23 Blast with a Backside George Reverse, like your life depended on it." But that's not what happened. Instead, I'm flipping through the playbook with my receivers, Thielen and Stefon Diggs, looking at our special end-of-game options. There's a set of plays at the back of the book that we practice every three weeks or so. But I can't find the one I'm looking for. "Where is that hook-and-lateral? I know it's in here. I just saw it!" We're all trying to come up with something, but there's no perfect play for driving the length of the field in 25 seconds with only one time-out. The Saints' kickoff sails out of our end zone. Time to take the field, but I still don't know where that hook-and-lateral card went, and so I just look at my guys, shrug, and say, "All right, let's just go give this thing a shot."

That drive didn't exactly start out in cinematic fashion either. Offensive lineman Mike Remmers, one of my closest friends on the team, had a false start on the first play. Then receiver Jarius Wright fell down on what could have been a big play. Another incompletion and we found ourselves with 10 seconds left, sitting on our own 39, out of time-outs. Throughout the season, we'd studied how long it took to get off another play if we completed a pass in the middle of the field and couldn't get out of bounds. *Was it 12 seconds? Fifteen? There's no way 10 seconds was enough.*

Being in the huddle with my teammates has always been very special for me. I still get chills thinking about having ten other guys locked in on my eyes, listening to every word that comes out of my mouth. Your world may feel like it's falling apart—fans are yelling, coaches screaming, the defense talking trash. But in those ten other guys you can see trust, respect, and love in their eyes. And I'll remember this particular huddle forever. Everyone was tired. We had fought so hard for four quarters. My receivers had run several deep patterns in a row, and they were *gassed*. The offensive line had been holding back guys like Cameron Jordan, a three-time Pro Bowler, all game. I told the guys the only thing I could muster: "This is it. I'm going to give one of y'all a chance."

The play call from offensive coordinator Pat Shurmur was "Gun Buffalo Right, Key Left 7 Heaven." Shurmur, who would be hired as the Giants' head coach not long after the season, made some incredible play calls that year, but this is one that nobody in Minnesota will *ever* forget. In fact, the next few moments still don't feel real. Pat Elflein snapped the ball and I dropped back with incredible protection. The line had been so good all season, and my guys were at their best right now, when we needed them the most.

I knew I would probably have to throw the ball to the right side. Thielen was lined up as the single receiver on the left side and had too much coverage. Of the three receivers on the right side, I had to focus on the one going the deepest. I saw Diggs flatten the angle on his pattern, away from the safety and toward the sideline. His route was called a Heaven 7—fitting for a play that many would regard as a miracle. I thought that if Diggs could catch the ball he'd be able to get out of bounds and stop the clock. I knew they would try to tackle him in-bounds if he did make the catch, but I had to take a shot. I took a hitch and let the ball go.

Sometimes the ball just comes out of your hand perfectly, and this was one of those passes. I lose sight of Diggs for a moment, but then I see these white gloves he's wearing—Diggsy is always very stylish—emerge out of the crowd. He's reaching up for the ball and I say to myself, "Oh my gosh, he's about to catch this thing!"

And he does. U.S. Bank Stadium erupts. It's the loudest I've ever heard a stadium in my life. But then I see Diggs turn and fall down with one hand on the ground. "Oh no! Get out of bounds! *Whatever you do, get out of bounds!*"

I've watched the replay several times since, but I honestly still can't tell you exactly what happened next. In the moment, I didn't see Saints safety Marcus Williams go for the tackle and miss completely. I assumed there were other defenders back there. I didn't know that nothing stood between Diggs and a game-winning score.

Everyone remembers the rest. Diggs streaked down field, straight into the end zone, threw his helmet, and the place went crazy. I couldn't believe it. I*s this real? Did this just happen? Wait for the replay . . . look for flags. (You never know.) No flags.* But then I looked up at the big screen and saw it again. No doubt. Touchdown.

Go back to the video and you'll see me running up to my teammates and yelling. Once again, these were not the words a Hollywood screenwriter would choose. They weren't words at all. *"Agghhhhggghhh! Agghhhhggghhh! Agghhhhggghhh!"* It was something between gibberish and primal screaming. My mind exploded. Forgive me if I didn't handle it like I'd been there before—I hadn't. It had taken a long time and a lot of work to get to this point. So many family, friends, and coaches had believed in me and supported me even when a playoff win like this seemed like an impossible long shot. I had to let it out.

I'm still running around, grabbing anyone I can find, when Vikings director of public relations Tom West grabs me and tells me I have to do a postgame interview with Fox sideline reporter Chris Myers. *An interview? Now? I can't put a sentence together; how am I going to speak to a national TV audience of millions?* But I said a quick prayer ("Lord, give me something to say—anything") and accepted that I wasn't going to be able to offer any kind of insight that could come close to matching the sheer madness that was still going on around me.

Myers started off with an easy one: "Can you describe the play?" *Uh, no.* "I don't even know what just happened," I said. "It's crazy." OK, not the most descriptive answer, but the words just weren't coming together.

Then he asked where this moment ranked in my life. It's got to be the best moment of your life, right? And that was a question I could work with.

"It's probably going to go down as the third-best moment of my life . . ."

Chapter 1

Playing for More

My dad's father left his family when my dad was a kid. As a result, my dad didn't have a positive male role model in his life when he was growing up. By God's grace, he got invited to a Fellowship of Christian Athletes huddle meeting by a coach at his high school. And at that meeting, he accepted Christ as his Savior. This led him to live a very different life than that of his own father.

The choice to follow the Lord changed his life and the entire trajectory of our family for generations to come. I'm sure as a seventeen-year-old kid, he wasn't thinking about the impact this decision would have on his future family, but without his faithfulness as a father, I would not have grown up into the man I am today. My opportunities to grow into a professional athlete, marry an amazing woman, and eventually raise godly children are in large part possible because my dad modeled what it looks like to be a man of God.

As I've grown up, I realize more and more how blessed my sisters and I are. After leaving home and living around the country, I draw back on countless lessons that my parents taught me. I can't imagine going through life without the foundation that I have. My dad's words *"Do the right thing, son"* ring in my head still today when considering situations. Did I always listen to them? No. But as time has gone on, I have learned that even if it's hard to admit, my parents were right about most things.

My grandfather started coming around again when my sisters and I started getting older and participating in organized sports. My dad had reached out and wanted to give his father the opportunity to be in his grandkids' lives. I have some good memories spending time with my grandfather during the holidays and at games, and I really appreciated him coming. As every kid does when he gets older and starts to learn more of the truth about the world, I slowly came to realize that it wasn't all rainbows and roses. My grandfather wasn't very good with money and he got involved with the wrong people time and time again. To this day, I still get phone calls from debt collectors looking for my grandfather.

I may not have had the best example of manhood from my grandfather. But my dad . . . he is a *stud*. It seems like every day I learn something new about Dad and come to admire him in an even deeper way. I'm sorry-not-sorry about being boastful here, but I have to brag a little about my dad because I think he is the best example in my life here on Earth of what our heavenly Father is like.

I realize that this topic is painful for many whose fathers were not around, who feel rejected or unworthy. I know there are many young men who have longed for the love, approval, and pride of their earthly father. While my dad was in the stadium for every athletic event, I know there are kids who are competing and looking up to the stands to find someone to cheer for them. The gift I have in my dad isn't lost on me, but even in his great love for me, he falls short every time compared to the love of my heavenly Father. That's the power, the secret I want to share with you.

If you remember one thing from this book, make it this: we all have the same heavenly Father who is full of perfect unconditional love that no human could ever give. He is waiting with open arms asking to be in a relationship with each and every one of us. That love, along with unbelievable peace and joy, awaits you. You don't have to earn it! He gives it freely. When you have this relationship like I have, you are eternally welcomed into a family that is far better than anything this world offers. When my father accepted Christ, everything changed. By the grace of God, my father's life was transformed and his heart was filled with love where anger had once been. In an incredible act of this grace, my dad took my grandfather back into our life and even took care of him in his final years when he came to know Jesus Christ as his personal Savior. What a story of redemption and victory. Pretty awesome. That's my dad. He restored integrity to the Keenum name.

He's a real man. He's a kingdom man. He's my dad.

———

Growing up, I didn't really think about how much money we had as a family. My dad was a coach, and my mom was a teacher. As a hard-working middle-class family, we never spent any money that we didn't have to. My brother-in-law complains about not being able to share a milkshake with my sister Lauren. She drinks the whole thing down the first chance she gets. That's because when I was a kid, if you didn't get your share when it was passed around the first time, it wasn't coming back to you. We went to Taco Bell on Sundays after church. This was a special treat for us. I didn't think about other restaurants I was missing out on. I may not have had everything I wanted, but I had everything I could ever possibly need and more.

The money I've been fortunate enough to make during my career will affect my family's financial situation for years to come. I find that money is very difficult to talk about.

Recently though, I've been convicted more and more that I can step up in this area of our lives. As our financial situation has changed over the years, I think I do a disservice to myself and the kingdom to not make my use of money a high priority in my life. The Bible not only calls me to lead in all areas of our relationship, but the Bible also mentions money more than heaven and hell combined. How we handle our money as believers is obviously important, so I want to make sure I am in line with Scripture every step of the way. I know I wouldn't be in this position without the Lord, and I'm not going to change who I am because of how many zeros are at the end of my account. I will keep doing what I'm doing, giving my firstfruits back to God—using the influence I have to support others who are using their talents to further the kingdom. Isn't all the money God's anyway?

> "For where your treasure is, there your heart will
> be also." —Luke 12:34

I've never seen a U-Haul on the back of a hearse. You can't take it with you. I've definitely regretted some purchases I've made for myself over the years. But I've *never* regretted parting ways with one dollar that I've given to church or a worthy charity.

> "From everyone who has been given much, much will be required; and from the one who has been entrusted with much, even more will be expected." —Luke 12:48

————

I've been blessed. In more ways than one. I want to share that with others. I *want* to get deeper into the business of making a difference. I have a platform through professional football. I have a unique opportunity to be part of something much bigger than myself. I can't imagine saying no to that. Just like I can't imagine keeping my faith to myself.

There is nothing wrong, in and of itself, with money. But my dad—and my mom—gave me something much more important than any of that. They gave me what I needed. They gave me a foundation of learning about faith that would guide me my entire life. They set me on a path that has sustained me, even when I couldn't see anything good up ahead. They put me in position to meet the One who would change everything about what I do, and who I am.

They gave me a framework to play for something more.

Chapter 2

Pray Hard, Play Hard

Abilene, Texas, is the place I call home. I was born in the small town of Brownwood, but if you know anything about football coaches, you know that they move a lot. And that's what my dad, Steve Keenum, did. In the midst of all that moving, if there was one constant in my life, it was football.

The sport is in my blood, always has been. Ever since I can remember, I've wanted a ball in my hands. Dad was at Ballinger, Brownwood, and Cooper high schools; and then Tarleton State University in Stephenville, Sul Ross State in Alpine, and Hardin-Simmons and McMurry Universities in Abilene. Growing up, I would find any excuse I could to hang around his teams, and a big chunk of my childhood was spent at the field house. Being a coach's kid was the best thing in the world.

I had unlimited access to the locker room, weight room, and practice field. The football facilities were my playground. From the very beginning of my life, I began working hard to be a part of the team. In those early years, I was working to be a part of whatever team my dad was coaching.

For example, when I got a little older, I asked my dad if I could be his ball boy—the little kid on the sideline helping refs during games. His answer? Not until I could throw a college ball from the sideline to the hash where the ref usually stood.

If you've never held a college-sized football, you need to understand something. Most kids my age were throwing a Nerf Vortex football that fit well in an eight-year-old's hands. But I practiced chucking a real ball—a ball that was bigger than my head, mind you—in the backyard every day. I kept working and working . . . and eventually it paid off. And once I earned that ball boy job, I didn't let go.

Saturday was the highlight of my week. Being on the sideline, catching extra points and field goals, being a part of big wins and heartbreaking losses—these are memories I'll never forget. Sometimes, when I'm back home, I'll see old highlights of those games, and there I am, running around the sidelines against teams like Howard Payne, East Texas Baptist, and Mary Hardin-Baylor.

I wanted to be around players any chance I got. One of my earliest memories is of my dad bringing me in front of his team at Sul Ross after practice and announcing, "If you can run a route and catch a pass, I won't make our players do harness pulls." Remember, we're in West Texas, and this was a typical scorching-hot summer day. Harness pulls were the last thing anyone wanted to do.

My dad threw the ball and . . . *I dropped it.*

I felt awful. But the guys on the team stepped up; they asked Dad to raise the stakes, double or nothing. If I didn't catch this one, they'd do *two* sets of harness pulls.

This time I really concentrated. I ran my route and . . . I caught the ball over my shoulder. I turned around and the entire team was chasing me! I guess I hadn't registered how happy they would be. I was terrified of these huge men running after me, and I took off in the other direction running for my life. When they finally caught up to me, they put me on their shoulders to celebrate. After I realized they weren't going to trample me, I felt like the coolest kid in town. My dad had the best job, and I was the luckiest kid in the world.

———

Being around my dad's teams, that's when faith and football really began to come together in my life. See, my dad didn't just recruit guys based on talent. He recruited men of *character*. Men who did the right thing. He expected his players to handle themselves a certain way. If you were on my dad's team, you didn't curse on the bus—especially when his son was tagging along for the ride. (I've been on a lot of team buses since then and, trust me, it's not easy to keep a bunch of college kids from cursing.)

I could tell, even at that early age, that certain players carried themselves differently than most. They talked differently, walked differently, on and off the field. I would come to find out that they were Christians. I still remember some of their names: Rory Peacock, Jon Rhiddlehoover, Wes Tidwell, Keidric Dixon, Johnny Golden, David Harmon, Brian Valenzuela . . . But McMurry quarterback Braxton Shaver was my guy. He was a great player *and* a man of faith. These men had accepted Christ into their lives, and they were living that out on and off the field. I wanted to be just like them.

Sure, we're talking about guys at a Division-III school in West Texas; they may not have been nationally known, but they were stars in my eyes. They were a great reminder to me that the way you behave as a player influences other people. What you say, what you do, even what you *don't* do—it all matters. I don't agree with Charles Barkley's famous line, that athletes aren't supposed to be role models. In fact, athletes were some of the first men I looked up to, and they had a huge impact on me. As people, the way we act matters. That's just as true for non-athletes as it is for athletes. You never know who's watching—a little brother or sister, a friend, a neighbor. We often underestimate our ability to affect others. You never know what kind of effect you can have by making a positive impact on others. You can actually affect *generations* of people.

The apostle Paul understood this. He wrote in a letter to a group of Christians, "Just one thing: As citizens of heaven, live your life worthy of the gospel of Christ" (Philippians 1:27). No matter where we are or what we're doing, no matter whether we're on the field or off, we should always live worthy of our calling. You never know who might be watching.

I've been fortunate to have a lot of great influences throughout my career, but my dad set the standard. He taught me what it means to be a real man of God.

Before every game, he texts me four things: *Pray hard. Play hard. Take care of the ball. Have Fun.* This is what I think Dad means:

1. Pray Hard. Faith is the foundation for everything. I play for an audience of One. Before every game, I pray: "No matter what happens, let my light shine for You, God." I don't just play for the name on the front or the back of my jersey. I play to glorify God. Life is too hard to go about it alone.

Playing QB is too hard without help. Prayer is our direct line to the Creator. Spending time in prayer is important not just before big games or big moments of our lives . . . an active prayer life means staying connected daily to the One who will always have your back. He's always there to listen. Take a moment to try it out.

> Rejoice always, pray continually, give thanks in everything; for this is God's will for you in Christ Jesus. —1 Thessalonians 5:16–18

2. Play hard. My pops is talking about mental toughness. Don't get down on yourself if you throw an interception or make a mistake. Give it your all on the next play. Nothing that happens on the field is ever as good or as bad as it seems. As Christians, we're called upon to maximize the talents that God gave us. We can't let the enemy distract us with negative thinking.

> Don't you know that the runners in a stadium all race, but only one receives the prize? Run in such a way to win the prize. —1 Corinthians 9:24

I learned a big lesson about playing hard at an early age from my dad. I was ten, and I was in my first year of playing Little League baseball. Tryouts were on a Saturday, and I was really excited. The tryout consisted of taking five swings at the plate, and then running to first base after the fifth one, whether or not you hit the ball. I proceeded to rip five base hits and, feeling pretty good about myself, I trotted to first base. Afterward, I went up to Dad expecting him to be proud. Instead, the first thing he said was: "Son, I don't care if you strike out, hit the fence, or get hit by a pitch—you run *as hard as you can* to first base." I remember those words like he said them yesterday. I don't run to first base anymore, but I still strive to play as hard as I can when I take the field, no matter the situation.

3. Take care of the ball. The football is the most important part of the game. And as a quarterback you have the ball in your hands every play. You have the most responsibility on the field. Accept that responsibility. Don't shy away from the fact that people are counting on you. If something goes wrong, don't make excuses. Do whatever you can to do better the next time.

I like to think I was a pretty good kid. But like most teenagers, I found trouble once in a while. Nothing major. There was the time my friend bet me I couldn't throw an ice cube from the stands at a football game into a tuba below where the marching band was waiting to take the field. (I *could*, and the guy playing tuba wasn't very happy about it.) Sounds funny now, but trust me: I paid for it later on.

In Dad's house, there was no getting out of trouble if you got caught. Which I did. One hot summer day, my friend Zac Taylor and I desperately wanted to go swimming. My family had a membership at the local pool, the Wylie Swim Club, but Zac didn't. So Zac and I told the girl working the front desk that Zac was Steve Keenum. Like that was going to work in Abilene—*hah!* Of course, the director of the swim club found out. He called my dad, and they came up with a punishment: I had to mow the club's lawn all summer long. As always, my dad was teaching me a lesson. Our actions have meaning and consequences.

4. Have fun. Football can seem like life-or-death. But it's not. Do I love to win? *Heck* ya. Do I hate losing? Probably more than I love winning. But we're out there playing for a bigger purpose than wins and losses. If you keep that in mind, competing can be an awesome experience.

In 2017, I was feeling really good in the third quarter of our Week 11 game against the Redskins. We were moving the ball well and the offense was totally in sync. I got into the huddle during a TV time-out and said, "All right boys, y'all know what? I'm having a lot of fun, let's keep it up." And what do I do next? I throw an interception to Washington's D. J. Swearinger, who runs it back to the 1-yard line. The Redskins score on the next play. So, I came out for the next drive and said, "All right boys, let's have some fun—but not *too much fun."* My point: You've gotta keep it loose. Despite the fierce competition, I've laughed and had as much fun on the field as I have in any other place in my life.

My father has somehow managed to attend every high school, college, and NFL game that I've ever started. That includes 57 college games and more than 60 regular- and pre-season NFL games. I know that, no matter what happens, he'll be there at the end of the game with a hug and a "Son, I love you, and I'm proud of you." He isn't shy with his football opinions. His insight as a coach is invaluable. But his lessons on life have had a bigger impact on who I've become as a man.

Of course, my development as a football player was a family affair. I've bragged a lot about my dad, but my mom, Susan, has been there every step of the way. If she's not at a game, I can count on a supportive call or FaceTime from her. If anything goes wrong, she usually tells me it's not my fault or promises I'll get 'em next time. (If your own mother doesn't have your back, then who does?) I get my athletic ability from Mom too. She was a Texas state-qualifier in multiple track events. My dad was an offensive lineman. Don't get me wrong; I *love* offensive linemen—no one appreciates linemen more than I do. There's just something special about those big guys—but when it comes to athleticism, I have to say: Thanks, Mom!

When I was seven years old, we moved to Abilene. And for a kid who wanted nothing else but to play sports, it was the perfect place to grow up. We were outside, competing in something *every* day. In fact, the only way my mom could get me to come inside and study my spelling was to make up a game. She'd give me a word to spell, and if I got it right I could run outside and shoot a basket. After I made it, I would run back in for my next word.

I admit, sometimes I went too far competing. I wanted to win at everything. I even got in trouble for cheating in Candyland and UNO. You might still be able to find UNO cards I hid in the couch back then to get rid of my hand and win the game. I'm not proud of that, but don't worry, my sisters caught me (sorry, Lauren and Allison).

My parents love to tell the story of when my dad was at Sul Ross, which has a very serious rodeo program, and my kindergarten class got to perform in a little play rodeo for the college kids. We got to ride broomsticks and pretend we were getting judged on our ability to control the make-believe horse. Well, I was trying so hard to impress the judges and win, I turned my broomstick into a wild stallion. I started out OK and then my broomstick got out of control.

I was the only kid in my class to get bucked off his fake horse. That ended my rodeo career.

My parents were supportive and encouraging in so many ways. They didn't believe in specializing in one sport, like so many of today's young athletes do. I played everything—football, basketball, track, baseball, soccer, golf, even gymnastics when I was really young. (I actually didn't start playing organized tackle football until I was in middle school, at twelve years old.)

I recently spent time back home with some of my former coaches—men who'd been wonderful mentors and set great examples for my friends and me. They've also been great cheerleaders throughout my career. We support our own in Abilene. We were standing around the track surrounding the football field at my old high school and went down memory lane all the way back to an eighth-grade track meet.

I was the anchor of the Wylie Junior High mile relay team in the district final, and we needed to win the relay to capture the district championship. This was the last race of the day, and all of the pressure was on me—just like I wanted it. It may have been junior high track meet twenty years ago, but it felt as important as the Super Bowl. Capturing that gold medal and helping my team win the meet meant everything to me. By the time the baton got to me, I was a good thirty meters behind. I didn't know how I would pull it off, but I was *not* going to lose. I took off and somehow made up a big difference in a hurry. At the very end, it was a dead heat. I still remember coming down that backstretch with nothing left in the tank. I gave it every last thing I had. I was neck and neck with the runner from the dreaded Sweetwater Mustangs.

Finally, I dove over the finish line head-first. I remember lying flat on my face when the judge came over to tell me we'd won the race. *Victory!*

I'm not bringing up the track meet to brag about my speed. I'm not sure I was any faster than any of the other runners on the track, really. But God gifted me with a competitive drive. It doesn't matter if the other guy is bigger, stronger, faster, or even better—I'm going to try my hardest to figure out a way to win.

As a football player you get measured up and down, evaluated and analyzed, all the time. But I'm not sure they judge the right things. The most important characteristics aren't on the outside. They're inside. It's what's at your core—what's inside your heart—that matters most.

There's a story in the Bible that shows us how God evaluates us. God sent His prophet Samuel to go and select a new king. He told him what family to go to but didn't tell him which son from the family would be king. So Samuel looked for the oldest. He looked for the tallest. The strongest. The most impressive. And what did God say to Samuel? "Do not look at his appearance or his stature. . . . Humans do not see what the LORD sees, for humans see what is visible, but the LORD sees the heart" (1 Samuel 16:7).

Those early experiences would set the tone for the rest of my athletic career. They taught me that it's what's in your heart that matters most. They were the foundation for how faith guided everything that I've ever accomplished.

My dad's players, my family, and my relationship with God formed me into the man I am today. If you want to get to know me—which I assume is at least part of the reason you picked up this book—you have to start at the beginning. I've been incredibly fortunate for a great start in life and to have been given a strong foundation. How would I sum it up?

Pray hard, play hard, take care of the football, and have fun.

Chapter 3

Under the Lights

If you're not from Texas, you might have some precon-
ceived notions about what high school football is all
about down there. Everyone knows it's *big*. Maybe you
watched the television show or movie *Friday Night Lights*.
You know the clichés: huge pep rallies, the whole town
getting behind the team, massive crowds under the lights,
cheerleaders, pickup trucks, and coaches giving inspiring
halftime speeches. Well, I'm here to tell you *all of that is true!*
At least, it was pretty close for me growing up in West Texas.

Like most places in Texas, high school football was at
the core of life in Abilene. It defined the community and left
a mark on both players and fans. I would be willing to bet
that if you asked a large sample of men or women in the
community, they would be able to name for you most of the
starting players on the local high school team. As for the
game itself, folks *really* know their football.

Take my wife, Kimberly. She was busy competing in her own sports—track and field and volleyball—but like everyone else, she understood football. Both her brothers played at the varsity level, and the game was a big deal in their household. When I signed with the Broncos this offseason, she actually asked my offensive coaches if we would be running the West Coast or a digit system offense. And those coaches were blown away—I'm not sure many fans know the difference between any two offenses. Simply put, "West Coast" means the plays are generally described with real words; "digit system" means that plays are identified by a combination of numbers. I was pumped to see how engaged she was. Keep reading this book and you'll see that's just one of many pieces of evidence that I married up. I out-punted my coverage, as we say.

In Abilene, the full-on football immersion starts early. In second grade I became involved in the "Adopt a Bulldog" program at Wylie High School. Wylie's mascot was a bulldog, and each year a varsity player is matched up with a little kid or two. As a child, this was the epitome of cool. You'd get to meet the player at a social function and hang out with the big kids, maybe throw the football around a bit, meet up for ice cream, or attend pep rallies with them. You got to build a connection with one of the players who took the field every Friday night. Of course, I actually wanted to *play*, even when

I was little. There was always a good pick-up game, or just a good old-fashioned bit of tackle-the-man behind the end zone on those Friday nights. You could be sure to find me right in the middle of every one of those games.

In fifth grade I went to Wylie's football camp and learned some of the fundamentals: how to get in the huddle and line up. We even learned the basics of the offense and defense that we'd eventually run at Wylie High. Wylie was still a few years away—and I wouldn't even play real football until junior high—but they effectively had us hooked on the program at a very young age.

Before I knew it, high school arrived. One day I was playing tackle behind the end zone with a bunch of other little kids; the next day I was on the varsity team. There's so much pride that comes with being a Wylie Bulldog. We truly hated our rivals Sweetwater and Snyder. One time, during a basketball game against Sweetwater, a kid on the other team was really getting on my nerves. I've never been in a fight my whole life. It's not my style. But I shoved this guy and got my first and only technical foul. Like I said, sometimes competition pushes me a little too far.

The highlight of my high school football career was spending so much time with my teammates. To go through all of those experiences with your best friends makes it so much more special. And I don't just mean during the season.

Don't get me wrong—fall in Texas is special. There's nothing like those Friday nights. But during the summer, *that's* when the real bonds were formed. Most of my buddies would work out in the morning at the Wylie Field House—or, as we called it, the Doghouse. We'd mow lawns or hold odd summer jobs in the afternoon, then go back up to the field and throw routes in the evening. And then find a pool at somebody's house to jump in. We'd keep the competition going all night with Ping-Pong or maybe a video game—*NCAA Football* or *Mario Kart*—at someone's house. I never was really great at video games. But let me be clear here: *I don't get beat at Ping-Pong.* That's right, Kyle—that's a challenge.

I took over as the starter at Wylie High as a sophomore. Coach Hugh Sandifer didn't typically start sophomore QBs. In fact, not many sophomores were on varsity at all. But that didn't intimidate me; I knew I could do the job. Ever since I was a young kid, I've loved to compete. And when I say loved to compete, I mean there is a *burning* desire inside of me to win, no matter what, whatever I'm playing. If there was any way to win, I was going to find it. We were a medium-sized high school in the 3A Division. For comparison, Kimberly's Cooper Cougars were 5A. They were rivals with Permian, the real-world school featured in *Friday Night Lights*. But in Texas, even 3A was ultra-competitive. After my first year on varsity, the team really came together.

My junior year we were good—*really good.* The upper-classmen were very talented across the board and my class-mates definitely bolstered our depth. In typical Sandifer fashion, we lost a few games during the regular season but kept getting better. We made the playoffs and really hit our stride. We made a run all the way to the state title game, which had only been accomplished one other time in our school's history.

In the state final we were major underdogs against Cuero High, which was far-and-away the No. 1 team in the state. But even back then, that was a position I was comfort-able with. The game was tight right up until the very end. Tied 14–14, we faced a third-and-11 at the Cuero 48-yard-line. I dropped back and no one was open, but I had to do something. *Anything.* So I took off for the sideline—and the defense assumed I was just going to run out-of-bounds. That's when I turned it upfield, around the left side, and scampered 39 yards, all the way down to their nine-yard-line. Two plays later, we had time for one last play—a field goal for the win. I actually begged Coach Sandifer to let me kick the field goal during the time-out. I had hit a 47-yarder in the first game of the season, but ultimately the job went to my teammate Tyler Driskell. Coach made the smart deci-sion by ignoring me. Tyler drilled it just as time expired, and the Abilene Wylie Bulldogs won their first state title! It wasn't quite the Minneapolis Miracle, but for a teenager in West Texas, that win was pretty darn cool.

There's no better feeling than being in the locker room after the game: blasting music, playing bumper cars with the laundry baskets, jumping up and down, yelling till we couldn't yell anymore. I also remember coming in the next Monday and peeking in on the seniors as they were having their final meeting in the varsity locker room. I heard them break it down as a team for the last time and I realized: It was over for them. It was also the first time that the same thought crept into my head: It's all going to be over someday.

———

The thing I remember most about high school football isn't a game-winning touchdown or a long run. It's that moment before the game, when you're done warming up and you come back into the locker room. Coach Sandifer gives his pregame speech and then says "let's bring it up." Then that noise of helmets snapping. *Pop... Pop... Pop... Pop... Pop* ... echoes through the room. Strapping up to go out there to compete with your friends.

Man, I love football.

For most of the players on a high school team, that's all they'll get. Our guys were so lucky to go out on a positive note that year. The emotional high after winning the state championship was incredible. But that's not normally the case. As good as we felt, it's not how playoff high school football ends for most people. Most teams lose their last game, and then it's just *over*. Almost every high school player in Texas has suffered the experience of crying after their last game. It's a rite of passage.

It goes so fast: all the workouts, all the practices, all the games, all the traditions. The pancake breakfasts that the parents put together for us on Friday mornings. The team dinners—the *whole team*, sixty guys, descending on some poor, unsuspecting restaurant on Thursday nights and eating everything the place has. The $3.99 buffet at Cici's Pizza was the best! The bus rides full of nervous energy with your best friends on those long stretches of West Texas highway. All those coaches who really want to help you be the best you can be. There are so many great memories that seem to last just a moment.

And then it's all gone.

My senior year didn't end on such an upbeat note. We were down 25–15 to Gainesville in the state quarterfinals and I knew: *There's no doubt I'm going to leave everything I have on this football field.* I break free on a long run from the Gainesville 38 and dive head-first into the end zone for the touchdown, bringing us within a field goal. Immediately I

knew something was wrong, though. Turns out I'd sepa-
rated my shoulder—my *throwing* shoulder. But I didn't want
to leave the game. I stuck it out until the very end despite
feeling a sharp pain every time the ball was snapped into
my hands. I even threw a Hail Mary at the end . . . but we
lost 25–22. It was my turn to see my high school career end
in tears.

But for me, high school football carried even more sig-
nificance—I didn't see it as the end. By my sophomore year, I
had realized I might be good enough to earn a scholarship to
play in college. Having my higher education paid for would
be a game-changer, and I was going to do anything I could to
make that happen. That meant crisscrossing Texas over the
summer to attend recruiting camps. I was kind of bummed
about that because I loved playing baseball too, but I had to
give that up in order to focus on football.

I went to all the big ones—Baylor, Oklahoma, Texas,
Texas A&M, Texas Tech. Around that time in Texas, you
didn't have to go far to run into a talented quarterback prospect. I would meet most of them at the camps. They were
from all different corners of the state, but we had one thing
in common: we had each grown up in a great football culture. Future Texas quarterback and longtime NFL player
Colt McCoy went to Jim Ned High down the road from
me. He was a year older, but that was a name I heard all

throughout high school. My future teammate in St. Louis, Nick Foles, was at Austin-Westlake. Greg McElroy, who'd win a college championship with Alabama, was at Southlake Carroll in Dallas. Dolphins quarterback Ryan Tannehill, like me, was in West Texas, over in Big Spring. The list goes on: Robert Griffin III at Copperas Cove, Andy Dalton at Katy, Christian Ponder from Colleyville Heritage in Grapevine, Chase Daniel at Southlake Carroll, Matt Flynn at Robert E. Lee in Tyler, Andrew Luck at Stratford . . . What an incredible pool of talent—and a bunch of good dudes as well. I always root for Texas QBs when they make it into the NFL, and it seems like two or three new guys are coming into the league every year.

There were also so many quality coaches—Hall of Fame-caliber guys who were legends in Texas. I was mostly aware of them because my dad knew them and talked about them when I was growing up. These leaders had a tremendous influence on generations of young men. One of the most famous high school coaches of all time, Gordon Wood, was from Abilene and attended Wylie for a bit. When he walked away from the game in 1985, he was the most successful high school coach of all time. I only met him once, later in his life, but Wood's strategy, innovations, and personal influence impacted thousands of other coaches and players. According to reports, he even made an impact on future

NFL coach Bill Parcells when Parcells was an assistant at Texas Tech back in the day. The list goes on and on.

I consider my coach at Wylie High, Hugh Sandifer, to be right there with the best of them all. He would always say, "It's never as good as it seems; it's never as bad as it seems." That's a great lesson on and off the field. Young men enter his program and become better players and better people. That's the most you can hope for from a coach. I knew the names of all the great Texas coaches: G. A. Moore, who eventually surpassed Wood's victories record and won eight state titles; Phil Danaher, who then topped Moore's record down in Corpus Christi; Randy Allen, who actually attended Abilene Cooper and went on to fame winning state titles at Highland Park in Dallas, where he coached a kid named Matthew Stafford; and Jimmie Keeling, who had great success at the high school level and then went on to match that success at Hardin-Simmons University in Abilene. My grandfather was actually a football coach too. My mom's dad, Orlie Wolfenbarger—that's right, Wolfenbarger—coached young men in the San Angelo area for a good number of years. Orlie, along with many, many more men like him, are the backbone of Texas high school football.

I'm very proud to have been part of Texas's football tradition. No matter what happens in my professional career, the state title will always hold a special place in my life. Not because of the play I made, but because of the teammates and coaches I did it all with. I learned so many life lessons on the football field, but coming together and trusting each other to accomplish our goals was the ultimate reward. I counted on each of my teammates to do their job and, just like Tyler kicking that field goal, they all delivered. My friends and coaches counted on me too, and I was able to come through for them.

I recently ran across a video of some interviews that my high school team recorded during my junior year, right before the state title game. Each of the players was interviewed individually, answering questions in front of a brick wall outside of Wylie High. In mine, I'm wearing a white, button-down shirt and a Looney Tunes football tie. (Yup, it had pictures of Daffy Duck throwing the pigskin. My good-luck charm.) In that video I managed to say something that feels pretty true to who I was back in those days: "Probably the biggest highlight of this year is hanging out with the guys. We got a great bunch here. We bonded real well. It's been so much fun. I can't imagine any other guys I want to spend four or five months out of the year with—night and day, sweating. It's been great." Cue the Explosions in the Sky theme song from *Friday Night Lights*. Roll the montage. Turn on those big lights.

Rewatching that interview today, I realize that even as a sixteen-year-old kid I was playing for more than winning football games. That silly high school kid had something in his core that he believed in, even if he might not have realized the extent to which it was there.

I believe we were all created by God, with something good that He prepared beforehand for us to do (Ephesians 2:10). I may not have understood it then as well as I do now, but football resonates for all of us—players, coaches, and fans—because it goes much deeper than first downs and touchdowns. We were designed with a capacity to bring God *glory*. The glory of football is just a shadow of something much, much more impressive than what we felt under the lights in West Texas.

Texas high school football will always be part of me, and I believe it prepared me for the next phase of life.

Chapter 4

Third Ward Cougars

He's not tall enough. Not big enough. He doesn't have a strong enough arm. I've been told that I don't look the part of a big-time quarterback going all the way back to high school. It didn't matter that I led Wylie to a state title. It didn't matter that I had a competitive drive or a great record. I just kept hearing the same things over and over again about my supposed shortcomings.

At registration for the Texas-El Paso camp, for some reason, I wrote down on the form that I was 6' 4". I was just joking—I didn't know anyone would read it. I quickly forgot about it when I went out onto the field. I was participating in drills, slinging the ball around, when I noticed UTEP head coach Mike Price was watching me, looking me up and down like something didn't fit. He comes right up next to me, and I can tell he's trying to judge how tall I am. I could've read his mind right then: *He sure can throw, but I don't think he's really 6' 4".*

According to Rivals.com, I was just a two-star recruit. I tell high school students not to pay attention to that stuff. You never know who's evaluating you and what they're looking at. People on the outside tend to see the externals only. Time and time again we've learned: That's not the best way to judge someone.

Nowadays, because of social media, everyone has an opinion, and recruits have to hear criticism from grown-ups who might be judging them solely on which school they choose. In our culture, what we *do* is often how we define who we *are*. So if what you do is throw a football, it becomes really important that you never throw it to the other team. If what you do is write books, it becomes really important that you get published. And if what you do is tell jokes as a comedian, it is really important to get a laugh. But the truth is, who we *are* is not what we *do*. We, all of us—me and you—are so much more than what we do. And when you are a college football prospect trying to make a college team, it's hard to remember that.

Fortunately for me, all it takes is one team that believes in you. That's a saying we hear used around the NFL Draft, but it's true at the college level as well. For me, it was the Houston Cougars.

Back in the day, Houston's coach Art Briles developed his spread offense to make up for the fact that his teams were smaller than the competition in the area. Earlier in his career he built one of the most prolific offenses in high school football history. Briles was able to see potential in me that other coaches didn't. And after my junior year at Wylie, he extended to me my one and only scholarship offer.

I was over the moon. After praying and talking with my family, I knew that was where I wanted to be. I verbally agreed go to play for Houston. And once you say you're going to do something in Steve Keenum's household, you're *going to do it*. I was heading to Houston.

———

When I've had the chance to play in primetime NFL games, one of my favorite parts of the broadcast is when you get to introduce yourself and say where you played college ball. I like to say: "Case Keenum, University of Houston, Third Ward Cougars."

The Third Ward of Houston is not a place where things come easy. The city is broken into six wards. The Third Ward is just southeast of downtown. It's a tough neighborhood, but it has a lot of heart. As it turns out, it was the perfect place for me. I'm very proud to have called it my home for six years.

I may not have been able to sit at a table with Oklahoma, Florida State, and Ohio State hats in front of me; I didn't make national headlines with my decision. But as different doors closed in my search for the right school, God opened the right one and put me exactly where I needed to be.

I redshirted my freshman year because of the shoulder injury I sustained in my last high school game. As much as I wanted to play, that year off allowed me to sit back and learn what college football looked like. Watching quarterback Kevin Kolb tear up Conference USA on the way to a conference championship fueled my desire to be a Division-I starter. By the next fall, Kevin had graduated and headed off to the NFL. I was ready to compete for his old job. But that's when something strange happened. Football, a sport that had come so naturally to me my whole life, suddenly became very difficult.

I came into the 2007 season positioned neck-and-neck with sophomore Blake Joseph in the QB battle. There was nothing I wanted more than to win that competition, and I put everything I had into the task. It consumed every aspect of my life. I started to become someone I didn't recognize. If I threw one interception in practice, it would ruin my whole day. I would replay every bad throw in my head and beat myself up constantly for what I could have done better. I was grinding 24-7. I was not a pleasant person to be around. I wasn't present for my friends and my family. I was short in conversations and really couldn't talk about anything other than football. It was all about me. And it was not fun.

~~Pray hard,~~ play hard, ~~take care of the football,~~ ~~have fun~~.

College was a very different experience from being back home. For the first time, I was on my own, making my own decisions. I could do what I wanted to, when I wanted to do it. And in a big city. I had much more freedom . . . and so many more decisions to make. But with that freedom came responsibility. In a new way, my actions had consequences.

Getting to church had been easy growing up. There are more churches per capita in Abilene than in any other city in the country—at least that's what we all claim. If I lacked motivation, my parents would wake me up to make sure I got there on Sunday morning. But when you get to college, no one's there to get you out of bed. It's a time when you make important decisions about your life, about your priorities. Are you going to wake up and go to church? Or are you going to sneak in a couple extra hours of sleep, or hang with your buddies?

So here I am, feeling alone and far away from home. I'm trying to win the starting job, but it doesn't feel right. I couldn't find the answers on or off the field.

I truly believe that God likes to make me uncomfortable so that I can grow. It's happened so many times in my life.

When things have gotten rough, I've turned to the one thing I knew would never let me down: Jesus Christ. No matter how many picks I threw or how many times I screwed up a play or misunderstood a coach's directions, God has loved me.

The Lord put a very special person in my life when I got to Houston: team chaplain Mikado Hinson. My dad had retired from coaching by this time, and he was working for the Fellowship of Christian Athletes, a group that is very dear to my heart. Dad knew Mikado through the FCA, and when I needed help, I was able to reach out to him. Mikado and I prayed together often. He gave me advice that I'll never forget. "Dude, you need to let the game come to you," he told me. "Remember who you are. You're a child of God, bro. It's not a performance-based thing. He's got you. He laid out a plan for you.

"Calm down and just play football. You're good. Don't try to be perfect. If you have ten plays and nine of them are good, don't focus on the one bad play. No QB is on-target one hundred percent of the time. If you're going to be successful, you have to let the bad plays go."

He'd nailed it. I was letting myself be defined by my performance on the field—and that's not who I am. As Mikado reminded me, I'm a child of God. Once I realized that, guess what happened? I stopped letting the bad plays get to me.

I stopped replaying practices in my head over and over. I stopped worrying about what my coaches were thinking. I stopped worrying about what the other guy was doing. I started having fun again. And not surprisingly, I started playing better football.

That summer, practice got a little easier every day. One afternoon, an assistant called me over and said that Coach Briles wanted to see me in the weight room. I walked in with no clue what Coach was going to say—and I don't know if he's going to tell me that I won the starting job or that or that I wasn't ready. Between sets, he sits up and says, "Keenum . . . you're going to play in the NFL for a long time." That *is not* what I was expecting to hear. I hadn't even played in a college football game yet. It was exactly the kind of encouragement I needed. It was also the first time the idea was planted in my head, that I might someday play in the pros. I was an NFL fan and had dreamed some day of playing there . . . but it was just that, a dream. Not a practical real-world reality I had spent time thinking about.

What Coach Briles *didn't* say is that I was the starter (Joseph, in fact, got the nod for the season-opener against Oregon, and I had to come off the bench). I would eventually win the job that season, but whether I started or not wasn't the point. In the process of struggling, of forgetting to have fun, of finding my worth in my performance, and then having truth spoken to me by Mikado, I had learned an important lesson about priorities. I am not simply an athlete who happens to be a Christian. I am a Christian who happens to be an athlete.

I don't care what your goal is—trying to win the quarterback job, studying all night to make a good grade, working your butt off to get a promotion—Christ comes before everything. When you come to learn and accept that, it changes everything. That doesn't mean that life is going to be easy and everything is going to work out exactly as you planned. But when you start living life in order to serve the Lord, your perspective changes.

> "Enter through the narrow gate. For the gate is wide and the road broad that leads to destruction, and there are many who go through it. How narrow is the gate and difficult the road that leads to life, and few find it." —Matthew 7:13–14

When I say that your identity in Christ comes before everything, I don't mean that everything else doesn't matter. The best part of being a Christian athlete is that we are called to excellence in all that we do. We are all given talents—unique talents that God specifically designed within each of us. As Christians, we are called to maximize those talents. Not just for our own benefit, but to glorify the One who gave us those talents. All things were created by, through, and for Him, so we do all things to glorify Him.

When I step on the field, no matter what happens, I want to glorify the One who made me. Whether I'm throwing nine touchdowns in a game (we'll get to that in a few chapters) or six interceptions (and that one too, unfortunately) . . . whether I'm throwing a game-winning touchdown in the playoffs or a game-losing interception, like the one I had against Colorado State in 2008. I always want to give glory to my God. I want to honor my Savior. Remember, I represent not only the names on the front and back of my jersey, but the name above all names, Jesus Christ. That's the reason I am who I am. That's the reason I play football. That's all.

The rest, as it turns out, would be part of college football history.

Chapter 5

The Show

In some folks' eyes, the Houston football program might not be as glitzy as the ones at Texas or Texas A&M. But man, it brought out the best in me. My teammates, the people who worked with the program, my fellow students—there were so many good people. And I'm not sure that any quarterback has had the opportunity to learn the game from better leaders. I had the honor of playing for *six* men who at one point were (or still are) Division-I head coaches: Art Briles, Philip Montgomery, Kevin Sumlin, Dana Holgorsen, Kliff Kingsbury, and Tony Levine.

It started with Briles, who saw something in me that no other college coach did. At the time, he was pushing the limits of the spread offense, and he needed the right kind of quarterback to make it go. I split time with Joseph in '07 but still managed to throw for 2,259 yards and 14 touchdowns. We finished the regular season at 8–4 and got to go to the

Texas Bowl to play TCU. It was a tough game, but I managed a career high 335 passing yards, and future NFL receiver Donnie Avery had 10 catches for 120 yards. We were in it to the end, but our desperate shots to get into the end zone in the final seconds failed, and we lost 20–13. The Horned Frogs had some freshman quarterback with red hair named Andy Dalton . . . not sure whatever happened to that guy.

Thanks to my spiritual growth and working with Mikado Hinson, the team chaplain I mentioned in the last chapter, my redshirt freshman year was incredibly rewarding. Off the field I felt like I had taken a huge step forward into God's light. I may have been far away from Abilene, but I was myself again. On the field, I set the school record by completing 68.5 percent of my passes. That was pretty cool. I was named Conference USA's Freshman of the Year and was poised for big things. There was only one problem. My coach and his high-octane offense weren't coming along for the journey.

In late November, Briles announced he was leaving Houston to take over at Baylor. Another challenge. I was going to have to prove myself to a new coaching staff. I had to make an important decision. Transfer or see who walks through the door to take over. I loved being at Houston and wanted to stay, but you never know what kind of chemistry you will have with a coach and what kind of offense they'll want to run. Ultimately, I knew the bonds I had formed with my teammates were deep. That was my new family and I wasn't going anywhere.

Any fears I had left were alleviated when the school hired Kevin Sumlin. The Oklahoma assistant coach had been around incredible QBs his entire career—from Drew Bledsoe at Washington State, Brees at Purdue, to Jason White and Sam Bradford at Oklahoma. Sumlin also brought with him Texas Tech assistant Dana Holgorsen. Oklahoma and Texas Tech had two of the most explosive offenses in the nation. *Count me in!*

Since it was a new staff, the quarterback job was up for grabs again. I competed and won the job during training camp. Once Coach Sumlin made his decision, he made it clear the job was mine to keep. I really appreciated him supporting me and communicating directly about what he expected. Turns out, I fit well with what they were trying to do offensively. My first game of 2008 I completed 33 of 43 passes for 392 yards, 5 TDs and 0 INTs against Southern. I was going to like this offense . . . a lot.

My next game was a bigger challenge . . . at Oklahoma State. They had a receiver named Dez Bryant that I had heard was pretty good. Um . . . yeah. Bryant had 236 receiving yards and scored four touchdowns. We fought hard and I ended up with four TDs and, once again, no interceptions. But Bryant and the rest of the Cowboys were too much to handle, and we lost 56–37. Still, I knew right then we could compete with a team like Oklahoma State. I couldn't wait to get another shot at the Cowboys and any other big-named school on our schedule.

In my first three games under Sumlin, I threw 13 touchdowns and just one interception. We didn't win them all—in fact, we started out 1–3 in 2008. But the team already showed that they had a special quality despite the early stumbling blocks.

Sumlin was a great teacher. Example: I threw that late interception against Colorado State that cost us the fourth game of the '08 season. On that particular play I tried to force the ball in somewhere I shouldn't have. Afterward, I was walking off the field—sulking off the field, actually—as quickly as I could; I felt I had let my teammates and my coaches down. I look up and Coach Sumlin is headed the opposite direction, right at me. *Uh oh, I'm about to get chewed out.*

But that's not what Coach Sumlin had in mind. He put his arm around my shoulder. "OK, you threw the interception," he said. "But what can we learn from this? All we needed was a field goal to tie. Then we can get the win in overtime. So what do we do *next* time?"

"Don't try to do too much?" I asked.

"*Exactly.* You need to trust your teammates and your coaching staff. We'll get this done together."

If Sumlin was a calming influence, Holgorsen brought the energy. He had a fantastic football mind and was a lot of fun to play for. He simply didn't care what the opposition did—we were going to run our offense and we were going to do it *fast* by getting the ball to players like Donnie Avery, Patrick Edwards, Tyron Carrier, James Cleveland, and Justin Johnson, and letting them do the work. I had amazing receivers. It was so fun to help them show off their talents every week. We would execute as well as we could, and then we would line up as fast as humanly possible and do it all again. The defense rarely caught up. In fact, we were pretty certain that teams started faking cramps and injuries to stop us from snapping the ball when we were driving on them. That really drove me nuts.

Holgorsen was also memorable because of his style. He was always drinking Red Bull and chewing Copenhagen. Whenever someone messed up in practice, his signature line was, "What's the matter, did you get drunk last night?" The offense was clicking to the point where that was the only logical explanation he could come up with for any kind of flaw. He was fearless, and his continued success—putting up plenty of points later at West Virginia—is evidence that his offense works.

Not long into the '08 season we started to turn the corner. We were learning to win. On September 27 we beat then-ranked East Carolina 41–27—the Cougars' first win over a ranked team in 12 years and first road win over a ranked team since 1984. Two games later we faced in-state rival SMU in Dallas. The Mustangs featured another star receiver, Emmanuel Sanders (I'll run into him later in the book) and could put up points just like us. Down 38–36, we got the ball at our own 15-yard-line with 1:58 left. We were in total sync that drive. The final play, I noticed SMU's defense was misaligned. My receiver Tyron Carrier noticed too. I gave him sort of a half-signal for a go route. Somehow, he knew what I meant and instead of running down the seam like we had before, he sprayed out toward the corner of the end zone. I was starting to learn that non-verbal communication is huge for QBs and receivers. I threw it over his left shoulder for the game-winning TD with just 24 seconds left. That might be the moment I was really convinced we could be special. Really special.

Later in the season we faced another ranked team, No. 24 Tulsa, and they didn't stand a chance against our offense. I threw a then-career-high six touchdowns and ran in a TD in a 70–30 win.

We didn't win them all. Rice—which was in the midst of its best season in years—beat us in our final regular-season game and cost us a berth in the Conference USA title game. But at 7–5 we earned an invitation to play in the Armed Forces Bowl against Air Force. The program was in a bit of a dry spell as far as bowl victories. The last one came against Navy in the 1980 Garden State Bowl. Fortunately, we were able to end that streak with a 34–28 win. We may not have been perfect . . . but you had to deal with a lot of fighters when you took on the Third Ward Coogs.

————

The offseason passed, and after months of lifting weights, watching film, and anxiously awaiting another chance to take the field, the summer drew to a close. It was football season again and we were ready to build on the success we had in 2008.

Flash-forward to September 12, 2009. It's our return to Stillwater, Oklahoma, to take on Oklahoma State. The Cowboys had just beaten Georgia to move up to No. 5 in the country, and Dez was on the cover of *Sports Illustrated* that week. They were riding high. But this was the game that we had been thinking about all offseason. Every time we got hot or tired during practice, all we had to do was remember we had Oklahoma State coming up in our second game. We wanted to prove we belonged right there with the major conference schools.

We jumped on the Cowboys early. Our defense was causing turnovers, and they couldn't keep up with our offense.
We went into the locker room with a 24–7 lead. We knew
we couldn't take our feet off the gas because their offense
was like ours . . . when it got going, it was hard to stop. And
Dez Bryant would not let up. He came out in the second
half and returned a punt 82 yards for a touchdown. By the
end of the third quarter, Oklahoma State was up 28–24. That
fourth quarter in Stillwater was electric. We went back and
forth exchanging the lead. We got into the red zone with just
under 7 minutes left and had one of the wildest plays of my
college career. I was moving around looking for a receiver,
ran into the back of one of my offensive linemen, scrambled
some more and tried to hit James Cleveland in the back of
the end zone. An Oklahoma State defender got his hand
on the ball and tipped it. It somehow ended up right in the
hands of running back Bryce Beall to put us up 38–35. We
went on to win 44–35. After the game, Sumlin said the win
"legitimizes our program." We had arrived.

After beating Oklahoma State, we were thinking big. Two
weeks later we faced another Big 12 opponent, Texas Tech,
this time at home. The program was starting to get some
attention. University of Houston's most famous alumni,
the guys from the Phi Slamma Jamma basketball team—
Hakeem Olajuwon and Clyde Drexler—showed up for the

game. I was standing next to Hakeem during the coin toss, thinking, *Oh man, this is the tallest guy I've ever been around.* Unlike the Oklahoma State game, we didn't start out hot. We were trailing the whole game. But we had a lot of confidence in each other and knew we could score when we had to. We kept it close enough to have one more shot in the fourth quarter. Starting out at our own 5-yard line trailing 28–23, our ensuing drive took the crowd's breath away. Receivers made clutch catch after clutch catch—including a fourth-down conversion by Patrick Edwards to keep the game alive. We got to the Tech 4-yard line with less than a minute left. That's when young assistant coach Kliff Kingsbury told Holgorsen that we should run a quarterback draw. Dana went for it. I motioned to empty the backfield, called for the snap, and ran it into the end zone. Final score: Houston 29–Texas Tech 28.

The draw was a gutsy call by Kingsbury. But I wasn't surprised. We had bold coaches. Kingsbury was the perfect addition to the staff.

————

Kliff Kingsbury and I had a special connection. From the moment I met him, he instilled so much confidence in me and took my performance on the field to another level. If you knew both of us, you might not expect us to have that kind of chemistry. We have very different personal styles. He's known for his perfect hair and cool Oakley shades; he's been seen out on the town at a cool spot or two in his day. Kimberly does make sure my hair looks pretty good, and I typically have matching clothes—but you won't exactly find me in fashion magazines. I'm more interested in a good meal or hanging out with the guys in a quieter setting than I am in going anywhere that has a velvet rope. But somehow, despite all this, Kliff and I clicked.

Kliff came to the University of a Houston as a quality control coach in '08. A former star quarterback at Texas Tech, he'd just finished a stint in the Canadian Football League, and I'm not so sure he'd given up on his playing career just yet.

One of my favorite things to do at practice was the bucket drill. Pretty simple—try to throw the football into a bucket in the end zone from different spots on the field. All the quarterbacks got pretty competitive.

Sometimes I'd hit four out of five and beat the other guys. Yes . . . bragging rights for the day. Until Kliff would calmly walk up, pick up a football and phoomp, phoomp, phoomp, phoomp, phoomp . . . dang. Five out of five. He was like one of the guys and encouraged us to have fun and be ourselves. But he also could put on his coach's hat. He let his guys know that he believed in them and encouraged us to be bold. It didn't matter if a play call was tough—if I had to throw it over a tall linebacker into a miniscule window and the receiver had to make a nearly impossible catch—if I said I wanted to try it, he would respond, "I absolutely love it."

As I started to get accolades that year, one of the best parts was sharing the ride with my teammates. We referred to ourselves as "The Show." We were good. *Really good*. We believed no one could stop us, and few did. But the best part about Kliff was that he also believed in me when things weren't working.

I was having a tough day in the 2009 Armed Forces Bowl against Air Force—our bowl-game opponent in back-to-back seasons. I threw an interception on a tipped pass early on, and then the wheels totally came off. By halftime I had thrown three picks. (For context: I had only nine interceptions that *entire* season.) I came into the locker room with my head down. Kingsbury, who was the quarterbacks coach at this point, typically sat up in the press box, so I didn't get to interact with him much during a given game. But then the first thing he does when he gets downstairs is get in my face. "All right, dude," he said. "I don't care if you throw ten interceptions today or ten touchdowns. We're not going to stop throwing the ball." The point: Kliff had my back. We were going to ride it out. And that we did. I threw six interceptions and we lost 47–20. It was a tough day. But Kingsbury's loyalty—his confidence in me at one of the lowest points of my career—meant so much. I've come to appreciate the people in my life who are there when I'm at my lowest. When you struggle together, a bond forms. The people I hold closest to me are the ones who have been there in good times and in bad.

———

A lot of people may not have believed Houston could beat some of these big-conference teams. We definitely were the underdogs plenty of times and had adopted that mentality. There was a lot of pride in calling ourselves the "Third Ward Cougars." Nothing was ever handed to us. Nothing ever came easy. We liked it that way. We wanted it that way.

In hindsight, it's easy to look back and see how God was working through it all. No, I don't think God has favorite college football teams (except for maybe Nick Saban's Alabama Crimson Tide). But I am confident He has worked in my life—I have seen it too many times to not believe. What is difficult to believe is that God *will be* working in the path that is right in front of you, even when you can't see. That requires faith. Hebrews 11:1 says, "Now faith is the reality of what is hoped for, the proof of what is not seen." Faith is looking ahead, without the benefit of hindsight, and confidently declaring the goodness of God.

God would have been just as good to me if we hadn't come out on top. The only reason I can come up with that things were orchestrated the way they were is that God is working on all of us—through last-minute touchdowns and tear-inducing defeats in the Texas State playoffs. But through it all, those with faith can declare His goodness, even when—especially when—we can't see what's up ahead.

Before the '09 season, none of us knew what lay ahead. Sure, we could envision success, but we didn't know if this season would be any different than the last. When you are secure in knowledge of God's goodness, you can look ahead, in faith, to rest—to rest in the way Sumlin wanted me to play—and move ahead with confidence. Without faith, you're a nervous wreck.

————

When I was in college I was introduced to Pastor Ed Young. Dr. Young has been one of the men who had the greatest spiritual influences on my life. His wisdom and generosity never fail to blow me away. After every game, win or lose, I know there will be two voicemails that will make me feel better. My mom and Dr. Young. Just like my mom, Dr. Young has the ability to overlook any mistakes I may have made no matter what happened in the actual game. The support has been there since day one with Dr. Young.

One spring when I was at University of Houston, Dr. Young called me into his office and told me there was a new game plan. He wanted me to speak at his church, Second Baptist Houston. It wasn't just any church. I was going to speak in front of somewhere between ten to fifteen thousand people in a weekend. At the time, I was not exactly a comfortable public speaker. I'm still more comfortable having a 260-pound defensive end chasing me in front of eighty thousand screaming fans than speaking in front of twenty people. Now Dr. Young wants me to get in front of all these people and speak for thirty minutes. I didn't know if I could do that. But once Dr. Young gets something in his head, you can bet *it's going to happen*. He didn't come to be the pastor at a church with over sixty-five thousand members by accident. He has a way of making you do what he wants. Not in a bad way. It didn't matter that I had never done it before. He pushed me and challenged me because he knew I had it in me.

The first time I spoke at Second Baptist, I was real nervous. Dr. Young comforted me by telling me that he still gets butterflies in his stomach when he speaks. Dr. Young always says that he can get up there because he's taught the butterflies to fly in formation. In other words, let God take care of it. For me that means just share my story. How I came to accept Jesus Christ into my life and how the Lord has done wonders for me ever since. Just like I'm trying to do with this book.

I've had the opportunity to speak in front of huge crowds at Second Baptist and also FCA huddle meetings with just a couple of dozen folks. It's always a very powerful experience. Mostly because I'm not really in charge. That's God at work. Not to mention the collective energy of the room. It's different than a football stadium, but there is that incredible sense of unified purpose. I'm so grateful for the opportunities that men like Dr. Young have given me, and the grace of God to put men like him in my life.

———

God puts certain people in your life at different times. Whether it is a pastor like Ed Young or a football coach like Kliff Kingsbury, you can bet God has put them there in the right place and at the right time. These men helped me become the quarterback, and the man, I was supposed to be.

Chapter 6

Down but Not Out

After beating several quality teams in 2009, we entered the '10 season with huge expectations. Some publications even ranked Houston in the pre-season top 25. Personally, I had my mind set on competing for the Conference USA title, possibly the national title—and definitely the Heisman race. I was even closing in on some all-time NCAA passing records. I thought this was going to be our year.

Turns out God had something else in mind for what was supposed to be my senior season. His plan was not comfortable for me; it was not the easy path. But, as always, it was bigger and better than anything I could have imagined.

We started out the season with convincing wins over Texas State and UTEP, rising to No. 23 in the AP rankings. Next up, a trip to play UCLA at the Rose Bowl. How cool is that—traveling to L.A. and playing on a historic field as a top 25 team?

That game didn't start out how we wanted, though. We put ourselves in a hole, falling behind 21–3. But once our offense got rolling . . . who knows? We could score a bunch of points in a hurry. We'd come back from bigger deficits before. In the second quarter I had the longest run of my college career—45 yards—to get us into the red zone. I was feeling good. We were going to score and start our comeback, I could feel it.

On the next play, I forgot the advice my coaches had been giving me and I tried to squeeze a ball into a spot where it didn't belong. The call was Blue Pop 23, and I was trying to find receiver James Cleveland in the end zone—but UCLA linebacker Akeem Ayers read my eyes and picked it off.

I would later joke that the lesson from that game was: Don't try to tackle a linebacker after an interception—especially one that would go on to be picked in the second round of the NFL draft. As Ayers started running toward me with the ball in his hands, he seemed to be getting bigger and bigger. (I was also surprised to find out he was faster than me.) But I was miffed about throwing the pick, and I didn't even *consider* backing off.

Ayers was taking it outside, toward the sideline, when he cut in to the middle of the field. I tried to change direction with him, and then . . . *Pop!* I knew it immediately. I remember lying on the ground, face down, for more than two minutes. I can still smell the perfectly manicured Rose Bowl grass. Doc O'Shea, Houston's longtime head athletic trainer, came over. But before he even had a chance to examine me, I told him through gritted teeth, "I tore my ACL."

————

With Doc's help, I eventually limped my way back to the locker room at the Rose Bowl. As terrible as the injury felt, I was glad to have Doc with me. He is such a good man. He even flew back to Houston and stayed with me until I could get my MRI at 5 a.m. the next day.

I was flooded with emotions. I didn't know how serious the damage to my right knee was, but I knew it wasn't good. I had a sense that our dream season was over—especially after my backup, Cotton Turner, came in to the game and fifteen minutes later broke his collarbone in multiple places. But it wasn't just our season going down the drain; I also worried that my football career could be slipping through my fingers.

I didn't know for sure that I would ever again play a sport that had been a huge part of my life since I was a small kid. It had consumed so many waking hours of my existence—dreaming about it, working to get better, competing and giving everything I had. *Now it might all be over?* The injury I suffered against UCLA marked the beginning of the toughest period of my football career. But little did I know at the time, God was working behind the scenes on other parts of my life.

Besides Doc O'Shea, the other man who didn't leave my side was Mikado. He leaned over me as I lay on the training table in the locker room and we prayed. That was the beginning of a hard period of work . . . both physically and spiritually.

Ideally, my doctors would have liked to let the swelling in my knee dissipate before they went in to repair my ACL, but there was also cartilage damage, and that required that they operate soon. I had no idea if the surgery would work. If I was going to be able to play football again, when? Would I be the same player I was before the injury?

I had an incredible doctor on my case. Doctor Walter Lowe was our team doctor, and it turns out he was one of the best orthopedic surgeons in the country. He said the surgery was a success. But I didn't feel like a success.

I had serious issues with the pain medication. At first, I was on a medication called hydrocodone. It didn't sit well at all. The pills and the pain made me throw up several times a day. For an entire month, the only thing I could eat was

Wheat Thins. I don't ever want to see a Wheat Thin again. I lost thirty pounds in the coming weeks. On top of the pain my knee was causing, there's no way I could play effectively at that weight. I wouldn't be able to generate any power throwing the ball and take the kind of hits a quarterback is exposed to. Losing that weight was not only hard on my body, it didn't help my emotional well-being.

Sleep was impossible. I couldn't get physically comfortable. More importantly, I temporarily lost sight of who I really was. I was depressed. I was making everything about me. *When am I going to feel better? When will I play football again? Where will I play football?*

As I mentioned before—if we aren't careful, we can define ourselves by what we *do*, and not who we *are*. At this moment in my life, I was believing the lie that we are what we *do* . . . and I was becoming nobody.

My mom or Kimberly would drive me by practice, still on crutches, and I'd feel horrible. I felt like I had let down the team. All I wanted to do was to be out there. I felt stuck.

One day Mikado was driving me around and I made him come into the facility to watch tape with me. I wanted to see the play. What could I have done differently? I was beating myself up pretty good. I should have called an audible. I shouldn't have tried to force that pass in there. Typical . . . trying to do too much. Ayers saw my eyes and I saw his.

I guess I wasn't much fun to be around. Because at this point, Mikado just looks at me and says, "Hey bro, when are you going to stop this?" Mikado knew me pretty well. He said he had enough of my depressed act. "You keep reliving this play. Stop." "I just want to see it one more time."

That was it for Mikado. "I'm leaving right now before I punch you, bro," Mikado said. "I'm leaving because I don't want to do anything that will damage our relationship. I love you too much." Then he walked out the door. I had to find another way home.

Mikado was right. And I knew it. Yeah, the 2010 season was ruined. Maybe my whole football career was over. But this wasn't who I was. I didn't want to live in the past and think about what I should have done differently anymore.

I often think that God likes to make me uncomfortable to force me to grow. I was definitely uncomfortable—physically, mentally, and spiritually. I was a lot more than uncomfortable; I was hurting. It took a long time for my knee to feel better and to be able to move around like I wanted to. I was also confronted with some hard truths about my identity. The thought occurred to me that if I'm not Case Keenum, the football player, *who am I?* Now I know that's easy . . . I'm Case Keenum, a child of God.

A few weeks later I thanked Mikado for our talk. "That was no talk, bro," Mikado said. "I was really going to punch you. I couldn't stand watching you sit there in self-pity."

One of Mikado's favorite sayings is a paraphrase of Proverbs 27:6, "Better are the wounds of a friend than many kisses of an enemy." His tough love was a big part of my recovery. It was time to get to work. It took time, but my knee started to feel better, day-by-day. Once I got my head in the right place, I could really get after it. Rehab for that kind of injury is painful . . . Like, really painful. I knew it was what I had to do. I didn't know if I was going to be able to play in college any more. Or if I'd even have a shot at the NFL. But I knew I had to try to put myself in position to play again.

Of course, this wasn't all about me. I needed help. I'm not great at asking for it. Like most guys, I'd rather try to figure out everything on my own. After the knee injury, that wasn't an option. I needed assistance with even the most basic day-to-day activities. When you're down like that, you learn a lot about the people in your life. I was about to realize something very important about one person in particular that would change the trajectory of my entire life.

Chapter 7

Kimberly

I had known Kimberly Caddell since we were little kids. We went to the same church and were in the same Bible drill. If you didn't grow up in church, it's like a competitive spelling-bee type event where kids memorize and recite Bible passages and locate passages more quickly than the others. I told you I am a serious competitor!

I was friends with one of her older brothers, Brandon, and growing up I knew her mostly as, well, Brandon's little sister. At that point she was just another girl with cooties that I mostly avoided. Fast-forward to my junior year of high school. Kimberly and I went to different schools in Abilene, but I ran into her at a Fellowship of Christian Athletes event. And my first thought was: *Whoa, she's not Brandon's little sister any more.* This pretty, tan-legged, athletic girl was somebody I wanted to get to know.

After that, I made sure we ran into each other at FCA events and at graduation parties around town that spring. Finally, at one party, I pulled my big move: I asked for her Instant Messenger handle. I know, pretty lame, and I'm dating myself a bit here, but it worked!

Eventually I got her phone number, and before long I took her on our first "date." After an FCA event we went to get snow cones. I had a buddy who worked at the shop and he would make sure our cups were overflowing with blue slushy goodness. We had a great time and I walked her back to her house.

Now, Kimberly has two older brothers, and while I was cool with Brandon, I was definitely intimidated by Brian. He was five years older than Kimberly, and he'd just come back from studying abroad. I'd heard all these wild stories about him running with the bulls in Spain and he had this European mustache. After our date, Kimberly and I walk up to the front lawn . . . and there he is. Even worse: our lips are both covered in blue syrup. *Oh no, Brian got the wrong idea!* We hadn't been kissing, I swear. But I got out of there fast, embarrassed and a little bit frightened.

Before our first real date, Kimberly and I were talking one night and she said she was going for a run in the park. I saw my chance. "That park?" I said. "This late at night? I better come with you." Before we even got to officially go out, we went for a late-night jog. Of course we had a great time. We always do. Having a wife who is always up for sports and outdoor activities is amazing. I think we're just lucky; we always want to do the same things. Not a bad reason to go to FCA events, guys—Christian girls who are into sports!

Before long we were dating seriously. Kimberly was a year older and she was going to Hardin-Simmons University in Abilene after she graduated high school. Things were going great—we couldn't get enough of each other. We didn't have to be doing anything fancy. Just being around each other was so much fun. Everything fit perfectly.

But sometimes, the Lord doesn't make things easy. Just as everything was going great, it was time for me to go off to Houston to play football. If you're not from Texas, you may think Houston and Abilene aren't that far apart. It's a six-hour drive. We were officially a long-distance couple. We lived in two separate worlds: mine in Houston, with my new football family, and hers in Abilene, with school and her friends.

We made it work the best we could. Kimberly came up to Houston on weekends, attending most every football game. I came home during the summer and any time I could shake free. But there was an emotional distance that came with our geographical separation.

I'm not really a phone guy. I'm not the best small-talker to begin with—especially on the phone. We both had so much going on, and it was hard to connect the way that we had when we were in the same town.

When you first start thinking about marriage and having a family, you tend to have an idea of how it's going to work. You'll graduate from college and get a job so you can support your family. I didn't want to be a married student. I wanted to be able to go to her father and say "I'm going to take care of your daughter and here's how." I wasn't ready. But then I got hurt, and God stepped in.

After Kimberly graduated, she moved to Houston to be closer to me. Being there was tough for her. Her life was back in Abilene—her family, her friends, her work. After graduating, she went to work for the FCA as an event-planner and absolutely loved it. The only thing she had in Houston, at first, was me. I still made time for Kimberly, but during college I was incredibly busy. My mind was on football and classes most of the time, which made me less available for our relationship. And she didn't seem to have the same spark living in Houston that she did before. There was something off. We were doing fine together, but not quite as good as both of us thought we should be doing.

But if there's one thing I can tell you about Kimberly, she doesn't stay down long. As she got comfortable, I could see her become less dependent on me and, frankly, more dependent on God. She went back to the relationship that had nurtured her throughout her whole life . . . the one with Jesus Christ.

We were working through the bumpy patch in our relationship and coming out the other side. Everything felt great, but I still wasn't quite all the way there. And that's when I tried to make a tackle on that Rose Bowl Field and everything changed.

———

Just days after we returned from Los Angeles I was in the hospital being hooked up to an IV filled with a concoction the nurse referred to as "the margarita." Well, I guess that cocktail of drugs was just the nudge I needed to open up. Turns out I'm a lightweight.

I was about to go under the knife, wearing my hospital gown, when I told Kimberly how I really felt about her.

I said I wanted to be the best boyfriend possible. I told her I loved her and that I wanted to build a life with her. It seems silly to me now, actually—I don't know what I was afraid of. But there in that hospital room, under the influence of heavy drugs, I was able to share my true feelings.

Kimberly asked the nurse, "Is he going to remember his speech after he wakes up from surgery?"

"Probably not," she said. That made Kimberly really sad.

But I did remember it, because I *truly* meant it.

The last few years of college I had been living with four football players and three dogs in a duplex we called "the Plex." The Plex was the last place on Earth anyone should be rehabbing from a serious knee injury. I loved those guys, but they couldn't provide the help I needed.

So after my surgery I stayed in Kimberly's garage apartment for a few weeks. My mom also came down to Houston and stayed on an air mattress at the apartment in the weeks after the injury. I needed all the help I could get. We were crammed in there. I couldn't move, I was having trouble eating, and even the most basic tasks were grueling.

Very early in our relationship Kimberly and I discussed remaining pure until marriage. We were young and very into each other. We could have easily gone in another direction. A lot of kids our age did. But it was ingrained in both of us that following God's principles about sex are a vital part of showing your love for the Lord. We dated for six years. Some would say that must have been hard, but we knew showing our commitment to the Lord would pay off. Of course, it also helped that Mom was there. If you could imagine how crammed we were in there, you would know what I mean.

I believe it has paid off for us, by the way, in more ways than one. Following God's way, especially when it runs against what it seems like everyone else is doing, pays off every single time.

It was a dark time, but even a slow-witted football player like me had to realize how much Kimberly cared for me. Here she was doing everything—driving me around, helping me to the bathroom, feeding me, making sure I took the right medications. And not because I was the starting quarterback. Not because of what I did. But because she *loved* me for who I was.

———

I eventually was able to take care of myself and I moved back out. The following January I was slowly starting to recover. It was a big time in my life and I wanted to share it with my best friend and the woman I knew I wanted to spend the rest of my life with. It was time. Time to pop the question. But I had to be smart about it.

Kimberly wasn't going to be easy to surprise. This was going to take a masterful game plan and probably a few audibles before the night was over. I told Kimberly now that I was feeling better we should go out for a meal to celebrate my recovery. Not bad, right? I thought so. But Kimberly seemed to sniff it out. I quickly got on my phone for reinforcements. I reached out to her mom and best friends to make sure they told Kimberly tonight was not the night. In reality, they were in their cars driving from Abilene to Houston to help us celebrate.

It worked. Maybe too well?

Kimberly seemed a bit disappointed that she would have to wait a little bit longer—she might have even shed a few tears. But she was up for a fun evening. We went to the Aquarium, a nice little restaurant downtown with good vibes. While I may be able to keep my cool in other situations, that night was tough. First of all, I'm not sure the atmosphere in the restaurant was exactly right. For some reason, there happened to be three children's birthday parties going on there that particular night. Great. Kimberly wasn't overly impressed. "Good thing you weren't going to propose to me here," she said. "This is a kid's place." OK, going to have to brush myself off after that one, focus on the next play. (By the way, they did end up hooking us up with a pretty romantic table that overlooked the fish swimming around in the giant glass tank. It wasn't that bad!)

We had a nice dinner. I was playing it cool . . . or so I thought. Kimberly knows me pretty well. She might have been able to tell I was up to something. She didn't know how much work I had actually put into this evening. On the way home I told her, "Let's stop by the stadium and see if we can get in." I'm not sure how much Kimberly had figured out at this point. Hopefully she just thought we were just going to have a little adventure. The front gate just "happened" to be wide open. Then we walked into the stadium and all my planning paid off.

I had arranged for my family to get to the stadium early for set-up. My mom and sisters had worked so hard to line up a row of candles that stretched from the end zone to the 50-yard line, leading to a table covered in rose pedals at mid-field. Sure, I had a little trouble getting down on one knee because of the injury, but I managed. When I asked the question, *she said yes.*

Both of our families were hidden up in the press box and they went wild cheering for us. The song "Better Today" by Coffey Anderson came over the loudspeakers. Kimberly was so happy. I was certain she was the one that I was supposed to be with. And I knew confidently that she felt that way about me.

That night, I gave her a new Bible with her future name inscribed in it. "Kimberly Keenum." I liked the way that sounded. I liked it a lot. I may have planned the decorations at the stadium and written a mushy note on the inside of the Bible, but God put us together and made sure we found our way into each other's hearts.

We were married on June 11, 2011, in Abilene. We scraped together just enough to get down to Sandals in the

Bahamas. I laughed as I told college football reporter Thayer Evans, then with FOXSports.com, "I've gone from having the least amount of sex on the team to the most!" It was worth it, trust me, and once again, God pointed the way. We honored Him by remaining pure and He blessed our marriage from the start.

––––––––

For me, marriage is sacred. It's the second most important decision you'll ever make. I remember hearing great advice growing up on how you should find someone to pursue in a relationship. It's simple. Chase after Jesus with everything you have. Pursue your personal relationship with Christ. When you're chasing, every now and then, look around to see who's chasing Him at the same speed. It may sound strange, but the key to our marriage is that our foundation is not in each other—it's in Christ. We are going to fail one another eventually. Every person is imperfect. We have defects. When you put two people together, you double the amount of flaws, and that certainly provides some difficulties. Only Christ is perfect. He will never fail us.

I love being married. I get to spend every day with my best friend. It was like that from the start. Everything is just better when Kimberly is around. I tell young guys who ask me about marriage that it's incredible to have a true partner. No matter who booed you during the game or if fans chanted your backup's name, to have someone on your home team who supports you *no matter what* is awesome. You can have the worst day ever at work, but if you have someone to come home to who's always going to have your back, life's pretty good.

After the wedding, Kimberly and I became kind of a thing at the University of Houston. Not many college students are married, so we stood out a bit. But everyone showed us so much love. Before every game the following season Kimberly would give me a kiss. And right behind me were Coach Sumlin and Coach Kingsbury to get their hugs. ESPN even came to the apartment and did a feature on our marriage. Fans at *College Gameday* held up a poster that read "Keeping up with the Keenums." Like "Keeping up with the Kardashians," but with a lot less drama. I'd like to think that our joy together had a positive impact on everyone around us.

So much of what you see about the institution of marriage in the press is negative. Kimberly and I want our marriage to point others toward Christ. In fact, that's exactly what the Bible tells us marriage was created for. Ephesians 5:32 says, referring to marriage, "This mystery is profound, but I am talking about Christ and the church." Marriage was meant to show people the relationship between Jesus and the church. And that's exactly what we want our marriage to do. Growing up we had some incredible examples of marriage in our own homes, and we want to continue that legacy.

I had gone to a dark place after my knee blew up on that afternoon in L.A. As much as I love the Lord, I couldn't understand it. I didn't know what was going to happen to me. But the experience taught me, once again, that the Lord is the only constant in my life. He's got me. He closed the door on 2010 and opened up the door to a sacred and wonderful bond with my wife. I was once again a very happy man.

Chapter 8

Chasing History

T he first hurdle I faced in returning to football was the NCAA. Shortly after my injury, I found out that the NCAA sometimes grants a sixth year of eligibility if a player loses two seasons due to injury. *Would they grant the extra year in my case? Was it time to seriously consider the NFL? Could I make it at that level? Would my knee return to full strength so I could even try?*

We quickly filed an appeal for a sixth year of eligibility. I thought I had a shot, but working against me was the fact that I had already redshirted my freshman year. And so every day I would run up to the compliance office on campus and ask if they'd heard anything. I'm pretty sure they were sick of seeing me.

If I'm being honest, I didn't think the NCAA was going to grant me that extra season. I knew everyone at the university was doing everything they could to help me—I'm so grateful to the friends, former coaches, administrators, and compliance staff who wrote letters and worked so hard on my behalf—but I started thinking about the NFL in earnest. If my request ended up being denied, I wouldn't have a lot of time to get ready for what came next.

I remember: It was a Saturday afternoon and Mikado asked if I wanted to drive around town and hand out FCA blankets to people who'd given money to the organization over the years. I was happy to do it for the distraction. I quickly forgot about everything and was enjoying meeting people and talking about FCA, when my phone rang. It was Sumlin. I knew Coach wouldn't call if it wasn't important; we would have just texted back and forth. And so I answered the phone hoping with every ounce of my being that it was good news.

The first thing he said was, "Well, we got it!" That's all he said.

I didn't believe him.

"For real?"

It was true. I got to continue my college football career. I squealed like a little kid. I didn't care who saw me, I was so pumped. The NFL could wait. I had goals left to accomplish at Houston. Now it was time to get to work.

About six months before I was injured, I'd happened to pick up Drew Brees's book, *Coming Back Stronger*. In it, Drew described how he hurt his shoulder, worked hard, and came back an improved quarterback. Looking back, I don't think it was a coincidence that I decided to read that book. My goal: to adopt the same approach as Brees that offseason. I wanted to come back stronger and be a better quarterback.

This wouldn't be easy.

The physical rehab work on my knee was grueling. There were days I felt like I was going nowhere, like I was hitting my head against a concrete wall. But if the physical aspect was tough, the mental aspect was even more challenging. My enemy was fear. *What if I came back and I wasn't as good? What if I got hit and my knee crumbled again?* What if I was never the same player again? I knew God would put me in the right place, but could I trust my own body?

I needed help, and it came in the form of Robert Andrews, a sports psychologist with whom the school put me in touch.

Robert and I worked on visualization, like:

> *What would the first hit feel like?*
> *How would I react if a blitzer came free?*
> *What happens if I throw an interception? Or a touchdown?*

I spent countless hours imagining the day I would step back on the field—what that would look like, feel like, sound like, even *smell* like. I really needed the visualization exercises to push through the hard times, and I've continued to work with Robert to this day, learning so much from him about the mental aspect of the game.

I'd like to say that I'm perfect, that I never waver in my confidence. But, of course, that's not true. No one has lived a perfect life except Jesus Christ. One of my flaws: Sometimes I need to see the outcome in my mind in order to go make something happen. It took a lot of work with Robert—and a lot of praying—to get to the point where I was ready to return to football.

God, it seems, has a sense of humor.

The first team on our schedule the year I returned would be . . . *UCLA*. Ayers had gone off to the NFL—thank goodness—but the Bruins were still loaded with future pros like Datone Jones, Cory Harkey, and some of my future teammates with the Vikings, Anthony Barr and Eric Kendricks. I still remember running onto Robertson Field on September 3, 2011, before the game, looking over and thinking, *Dang, they're big. Really big.* But we were fast, and I couldn't wait to get back at it. The Show was back.

In the end, that day went even better than I had visualized with Robert. We opened with a 16-play scoring drive. I was so happy that, running back to the sideline, I tried to high-five and hug all the people who'd helped me come back stronger. There were so many people: coaches; administrators; Dr. Walter Lowe, the orthopedic surgeon who worked on my knee; all the trainers who spent hours with me, rehabbing; Doc O'Shea, who encouraged me every day; Hideyuki Okuwa, the trainer whose magic hands soothed my sore knee after every grueling workout; world-renowned physical therapist Russ Paine, trainers Jon Houston and Andrew Crane . . . And many, many others. I wanted to share my joy with *all* of them.

I ended up completing 30 out of 40 passes that day for 310 yards and two touchdowns in a hard-fought 38–34 win. Afterward, UCLA coach Rick Neuheisel came up to me and told me that was one of the greatest performances he'd ever seen from a quarterback—and this from a guy who's been involved in the college or pro game since 1980.

With that first contest out of the way, it was time to get rolling. One of the most disappointing effects of my injury was the thought that I would never break the NCAA records that I'd been so close to reaching in the 2010 season, and I didn't want to lose the opportunity to make my mark on the sport. Now that I was healthy, back with my teammates, nothing was going to stop us.

We were putting up big numbers. *Really big*. Like, numbers no one had ever seen before. Everyone was on the same page and our offense was working perfectly. On October 27, I threw nine touchdowns in a 73–34 win over Rice. (Believe it or not, it was raining that day.) Patrick Edward caught five touchdowns in that game alone—that's right, *five*—and had over 300 yards receiving. That performance left me just 267 yards behind Hawaii's Timmy Chang for the all-time record, and we still had five games to go.

We next played at Alabama-Birmingham on a Saturday night, November 5. But if I was expecting loads of national attention, I wasn't going to get it. As luck would have it, that season's version of the Game of the Century was going on at the same time: No. 1 LSU against No. 2 Alabama. In fact, most of the people at Legion Field were more focused on getting Crimson Tide score updates than they were on what was happening right in front of them.

I set the record in the third quarter with a 16-yard pass to Justin Johnson. You might think they'd have stopped the action and celebrated. Who knows, maybe fireworks? Perhaps the head of the NCAA would come out and lead some sort of ceremony? *Nope.* None of that happened. Not that we had time for it. We were running fast tempo, and we didn't slow down for anything. Our approach was: on to the next play, and the next, and, before long, the end zone. In fact, as we were marching down the field, apparently our equipment manager was frantically running around, trying to make sure he had the football that set the record.

There wasn't much in terms of pomp and circumstance, and I wouldn't have had it any other way, really. If the national media was focused elsewhere, that was OK. As teammates, we were playing for each other that season—winning games and smashing records together. And boy was it fun. In the end, we finished the regular season 12–0 and climbed all the way up to No. 7 in the AP rankings.

The only remaining obstacle that stood between us and a BCS bowl game was Southern Miss in the Conference USA title game.

The Golden Eagles and their quarterback, Austin Davis (another future teammate with the Rams), beat us 41–27, ending our hopes of playing in the Sugar Bowl. It was one of the toughest losses of my career, and I was feeling really down after the game.

I'd brought a huge entourage to the stadium, including my seventh-grade basketball coach. I'd promised Coach Bacon that I'd take his son, Duncan, down to the locker room after the game—but that was the last thing I wanted to do when that moment finally came. Dad had taught me to honor my commitments, though, and sure enough, Duncan was still up for the locker room, even though we'd lost. I took him in to meet some of the guys, who were also down in the dumps. Then a funny thing happened.

Duncan didn't care that we'd lost. He was so happy just to be with us. In fact, he told me it was one of the coolest things he'd ever done. His positivity was contagious and he knocked me out of my little funk. Ultimately, his joy meant more to me than the personal glory I was hoping for that night. Once again I was reminded that athletes have a real influence on young people.

After that loss to Southern Miss, we were off to face Penn State in the Ticket City Bowl. Kliff gave me a nice going-away present for the season: a game plan with only one running play! I completed 45 of 69 passes for 532 yards and three touchdowns. I even set the record for the most passing yards in one quarter of a bowl game, 227. It was the perfect way to end my playing career at Houston. After the game I even went up into the stands and tried my best to lead the band in our school's fight song.

After the season wound down, I had the honor of going on the awards banquet circuit. Win or lose, those are always fun because you get to meet cool people and talk football. But they also come with their odd moments.

At the Davey O'Brien Award ceremony, where they honor the top collegiate quarterback, one reporter came up to me and said, "I'm not sure if I'm supposed to tell you this, but I just wanted you to know: I have a vote—and I voted you third." *OK.* Was that supposed to make me . . . *happy?*

"You know I'm one of the three finalists, right?" I asked.

I wasn't mad. I'd gotten over being upset at people who underestimate me. It had been happening my whole career. And the people who vote on these awards, they didn't know me; they weren't the people I should have been focusing on. My teammates, my coaches, my family, and my friends— that's who mattered most. People like Duncan, who was so grateful that I would include him. The people who'd helped me get back on my feet after the knee injury and reach this sixth and final season. The Houston fans who were with me from the beginning.

Robert Griffin III won the Davey O'Brien Award that night, and eventually the Heisman Trophy as well. I came in seventh in that Heisman race behind him, Andrew Luck, and a handful of other future NFL players. Of course, I'm a competitor. I wanted to win! But in the end, it wasn't the most important thing. I came a long way at Houston. I wouldn't trade my time in the Third Ward for time at any other school in the country. I learned a lot, grew into a man, and married my best friend. I laughed, cried, and had a ton of fun. And I will *always* rep H-Town hard.

———

Just in case you think that this is the part of the story where I get a big head, don't worry. I have lots of people I grew up with to help me stay humble. And just in case, God always gives me little reminders.

After my final season at the University of Houston, I got to travel to Indianapolis for the festivities surrounding Super Bowl XLVI. This is a big week in the sports business. Players get to make business connections and arrange endorsement deals. On Wednesday, Thursday, and Friday before the game, I hopped from interview to interview on "Radio Row" and met cool football fans from all over the country. It can be a lot to handle, but most of it is really fun. As the weekend approaches, everyone starts talking about the parties. "You headed to the EA Sports party? What about Sports Illustrated? I heard Zac Brown is at the Pepsi party."

I was feeling pretty good because I got a special invitation to the ESPN "Next" event on Saturday night. I was excited to see what all the fuss was about. They even offered to pick me up in a limousine and drop me off at the front door. But I had already committed to attending a peewee football clinic across town and would have to hustle over the party late. I got a ride with my new marketing representative and soon-to-be very close friend Dusty Stanfield in his rented Nissan sedan. Not exactly a limo.

We pulled up to a parking lot that was right next to the front door of the venue and were immediately stopped by an anxious attendant.

"You can't park here," she said, somewhat urgently because the whole scene out front was a madhouse.

"You don't unterstand," Dusty said, "I have Case Keenum in the car."

"Who?"

"Case Keenum. You know, college football's all-time leader in passing yards?"

Nothing.

"He also led in touchdowns and completions."

"Who?"

She looks real hard over Dusty's shoulder to try to figure out who I am. I'm shrinking down in my seat with embarrassment, and she definitely doesn't recognize me, but those records sound important enough for her to get her manager. OK, he'll clear this up and get me going to the party with the other A-listers.

The manager walks up and says, "Who are you dropping off?"

"Case Keenum," Dusty pleads. "You know . . . *Case Keenum.*"

Looks like we're going 0-for-2. He just stares at our car blankly. Dusty takes over. He's throwing out facts and figures about my football career rapid fire. He might have even made up a few things, but Dusty has an ability to talk his way into anything. He made it sound like the party couldn't start until LeBron James, Derek Jeter, and Case Keenum showed up.

Either the attendants were impressed or they just wanted to get on with their night. "Go on through, Mr. Keenum (*whoever you are*)."

The party was cool, by the way.

I got to walk a red carpet for the first time and hear Drake perform. We ended up spending most of the night hanging with former *Saturday Night Live* cast member and *Last Man on Earth* star Will Forte, who was a great guy and actually knew a ton of football.

My success at Houston raised my national profile to a *certain* level—but only to a certain level. Probably because we played in Conference USA, not a power-five conference, or because we just missed out on a BCS bowl game. Maybe because I was never invited to the Heisman ceremony. But I honestly didn't mind. Regardless of all that, after six years, it was time to continue down the path that God had laid out for me—the draft and a career in professional football. That low profile was about to change in the NFL . . .

At least, I sure hoped so.

Chapter 9

Draft Daze

When you arrive at the NFL scouting combine in Indianapolis—the annual convention where teams get to look at prospective players for their teams up close—the very first thing each player gets is a schedule card, and on the back is a list of all your private meetings with teams. I eagerly grabbed my card, flipped it over, and ... it was blank. Not a single team wanted to sit down and get to know me better. Maybe they'd seen enough of me in six years of college. Maybe they just weren't interested at all.

Not exactly a confidence-builder.

I run into trouble when I overanalyze situations. I try to figure out every angle and, typically, I drive myself nuts. When I was rehabbing from my knee injury, Robert Andrews talked to me about striving for excellence instead of look-ing for perfection. When I get stuck on perfection, I focus too much on not making mistakes. But when I think about excellence, I'm in a mind-set to be better every day, regardless of whether I fail or succeed. When things are going well, I'm relaxed, relying on my God-given talents. I'm not consumed by the results as much as I'm enjoying the process.

I was absolutely *grinding* leading up to the draft. And I was constantly worried. *Am I doing enough to prepare?* I worked out twice each day, trying to do anything I could to impress people. But I wasn't *enjoying* the process. It wasn't much different from my early days at Houston, to be honest. I didn't feel like myself.

When the combine finally arrived, I was nervous. And not an excited nervous, like I get before games, when I know I'm prepared. Nervous like: *Man, I better not screw up in front of all these NFL coaches.*

To make matters worse, I line up for the 40 and guess who's running right in front of me: Robert Griffin III. The guy ran a 4.41—the fastest 40 time for a quarterback in combine history. And me? I ran a 4.79 on my first try, and then I tweaked my hamstring trying to push the limits on my second attempt. Safe to say, RGIII's record was plenty safe. Robert is a world-class track athlete and QB, so I don't feel too bad. But my days of winning races had ended (flat on my face) back on that track in junior high.

After I pulled my hamstring, I didn't participate in any of the other measured physical tests. I did, however, decide to throw in the passing drills. *Typical of me, trying to do too much.* I can't completely blame my tight hamstring. I was mentally tight too. I lined up for one of my first throws of the day, a simple 12-yard curl route—one I'd completed a thousand times before, with a lot more pressure, and with grown men chasing after me. But on this occasion, I dropped back and proceeded to sail the ball five yards over my receiver's head. He didn't even jump for it—it was that far off. Now, no one overthrows a curl route. You overthrow a deep post or a corner route. That's the kind of day I had in Indianapolis.

I returned to Houston unsure of where I stood. *Would I be drafted? If not, where would I end up? Was it possible that my playing days were over?* The lack of interest from teams in the subsequent weeks did little to calm me. No team asked me to fly across the country for a visit. In my worst moments I was starting to get shaken about my ability; I started to wonder whether I'd even get a shot to play at the next level.

Satan can be sneaky when it comes to negative thinking. If you're not vigilant, those damaging thoughts can creep in and find a home in your head. The Bible warns us about this. It tells us we have to take control of our minds. It tells us to focus on things that are pure, commendable, and praiseworthy, not to focus on negative things (Philippians 4:8). But we all know how easy it is to fall into that negative cycle. The Bible says. "Your adversary the devil is prowling around like a roaring lion, looking for anyone he can devour" (1 Peter 5:8).

One day I took a break from training to play golf with my brother-in-law, Brian. Yup, the same intimidating brother-in-law I met the night of my first date with Kimberly, with my suspiciously blue mouth. He'd warmed up to me over the years. We play golf all the time now, and it seems like he's always letting me win. Who knew he was such a nice guy?

I'm at the range warming up for our round and he comes up to me with an excited look on his face. "Dude, I saw Gary Kubiak in the clubhouse. Let's go say hello."

Maybe I wasn't feeling good about myself at the time, but I really didn't want to talk to the Houston Texans' head coach at that moment. "Naw, he's here to have fun," I said. "We're not going to bother him."

"All right, fine. But I think we should," he said back.

"Let's just play golf."

Well, we pull up to the first tee and who's standing there? *Gary Kubiak.* We said hello, and he couldn't have been any friendlier. He asked if we wanted to play through. And that's when Brian blurts out—without my consent, mind you— "Yeah, that'd be awesome." *Great. Now I have to hit my first drive in front of Coach Kubiak. What if I get tight, like at the combine?*

My brother-in-law gets up there and hooks it into the woods. Not a good showing to start. *Now, please don't let me hit a dribbler—the golf equivalent of some of the throws I missed in Indianapolis.* And then something funny happened. It's like I just got tired of worrying. I'd already disappointed myself at the combine. It couldn't get any worse. I approached the ball and . . . *Bang!* I crushed it—one of the longest, straightest drives of my life.

"I guess *all* quarterbacks are good at golf," Kubiak joked.

I saw Kubiak a few days later when I was invited to a workout that the Texans were holding for prospects from colleges in the area, and I threw really well that day. I still remember the little things Kubiak pointed out to me. I was having trouble getting used to lining up under center, after having played in the shotgun throughout college. "Case, stay a little higher at the back of your drop," he told me. "Hang on your back foot a little longer on this route to let the wide receiver work open." The ball just *popped* out of my hand that afternoon. Months later, Kubiak told me that if I'd thrown like that at the combine, I would have easily been drafted. But like I said earlier, it seems the Lord has a sense of humor.

––––––––

Not every part of the pre-draft process was a total drag. One of the highlights was appearing on Jon Gruden's *QB Camp.*

Before he ever decided to return to coaching with the Raiders, Gruden used to interview some quarterback prospects for a show on ESPN. Now that I have to play him twice a season, I probably shouldn't say anything nice about Coach, but I always enjoy seeing him, and I've appreciated the kind words he's said about me when he's called my games on *Monday Night Football*. Coach Gruden and I broke down some of my film from Houston, focusing on some negative plays, including a few big hits. At one point he pulled up a play where a defensive back from SMU drilled me near the sideline.

"This is insane right here," he said. "Explain yourself."

"I see the sticks and I'm trying to get to them," I said. "That guy came out of nowhere. I'm trying to get out-of-bounds. He does lay a pretty good hit on me there."

"You think?"

Lucky for me, Coach quickly turned to some tape that I liked a lot more. And if you've watched Monday Night Football over the years, you'll recognize the way he talks: "You know what I love about you, Keenum? You've got some serious guts, man. Some of these throws you made from awkward body positions, guys beating right down on you—these are some of my favorite plays. Not many guys can stare down the gun barrel like this and throw a strike.

"Bro, that's a *great* throw. They're coming at you with a stunt dog right up the middle. A lot of people would have bailed. A lot of people would have crumbled. Know what I would have done? I would have said, 'Hey, punt team!' That's a big-time throw." Now we were cooking.

Next Gruden showed me a clip of an unrecognizable quarterback in a blue-and-white uniform. The QB evaded a couple of rushers and threw a perfect strike down the field on the run. It was weird, because this guy sure looked like someone who could play big-time college football . . . but I couldn't place him. Eventually Gruden revealed: It was Tony Romo, the Eastern Illinois quarterback who went undrafted in 2003 and landed with the Cowboys, where he started 127 games.

"Does the draft *really* matter?" Gruden asked. "I'll bet you a Coke that you can't name the top three picks in the draft two years ago. At the end of the day, at the end of your career, at the end of time: Does it really matter? No. All it takes is one coach that believes in you. Just be ready. Just be ready. Just be ready. Because you will get your chance. You're going to be alright, Keenum."

Coach Gruden's advice was prophetic. I sat through the whole draft without hearing my name called. We spent the day at our cousins' house. I was trying to keep busy the whole time. But I basically just nervously paced throughout the house and outside. All right, God was putting another challenge in front of me. I wasn't happy, but I'd been there before.

I didn't have long, though, to sit and think about what it meant, not being drafted. Just a few minutes after the last pick, my phone rings. It's Karl Dorrell, the Texans' quarterbacks coach, and Houston wants to sign me as an undrafted free agent. I guess that drive I hit in front of Coach Kubiak really made an impression.

Once again, God had closed several doors, but He left the right one open for me—all I had to do was walk through. I could have been drafted by a team in the seventh round and shipped off to a situation that wasn't the right fit. Instead, I got to stay in a city that had embraced me for the past six years. I didn't get to travel to New York and hug the commissioner on draft day. But God had a plan, as He always does.

Chapter 10

Welcome to the NFL

Entering the NFL is challenging for any player, but especially so for a quarterback. I was in for some big changes coming out of Houston. A pro-style offense is quite different from what the Cougars were running. Honestly, I didn't even know *what I didn't know* at that point. I had to learn an entirely new language, essentially. The pro playbook is quite extensive, and I struggled to wrap my head around the whole thing.

Guess what: some of those same issues I'd suffered from before the draft, they crept into my first NFL offseason too. I found myself thinking too much, searching for perfection rather than just striving for excellence. I'll try to be fair to myself here and assume that most quarterbacks coming into the league don't understand the nuances of the game; I certainly didn't.

Quarterback is a cerebral position, even more so than in college. There are so many decisions you need to make, pre- and post-snap. Everything has to be second nature. You can't stop to think even for a millisecond. If you have to speed up your drop because you're going to be throwing a stop route to the left, you just do it. *Pop-pop-pop-pop-pop*—five quick steps and throw. If you're tempo'ing your drop to throw a comeback and you want to read the coverage on the front side before you get back to the other side, then you might slow your drop down. *Da . . . da . . . da . . . da . . . da . . . da . . . da*—then hitch and throw.

Learning the fundamentals of the pro game is something that's taken me time. In fact, I'm still learning. Guys like Tom Brady, Aaron Rodgers, and Drew Brees operate at such a high level because they're not thinking. The basic mechanics of the position are like breathing to them. It's very hard for young QBs to come into the league and succeed early. Major props to those who have.

So, with the Texans, I found myself an undrafted free agent sitting in a room with three other quarterbacks, all of us competing for three spots. Ahead of me were Matt Schaub, who'd led the NFL in passing yards in 2009. Then came T. J. Yates and John Beck, both of whom were young but had experience in the league. I was the young gun trying to prove myself.

Starting over in the pros would prove a humbling experience. There was just so much to learn. I tried my best to catch up with the snaps I got in practice. And I even got to play a little bit in the preseason. Didn't throw any picks, which was a good thing. Problem is, I didn't throw any touchdowns either. I was not shocked after the last exhibition game that I didn't make the team. But on cut day, Coach Kubiak, who has always been in my corner, told me they were placing me on the practice squad—basically, a group of eight to ten guys who aren't on the *actual* team but who still practice and go to work every day with the team. That meant I would get to learn the game while doing whatever I could at practice to help the team.

I got almost zero quarterback reps while on the practice squad. Sometimes I even had to play defensive back on the scout team—I even had to cover Andre Johnson, a seven-time Pro Bowler. I can't say that I was any good at that. I just tried my best to stay out of his way; I didn't want to hurt anyone—plus, I remembered what happened when I tried to make that tackle against UCLA. I wanted to eventually throw to this guy!

Most of my reps that season were of the mental variety. Schaub got the first-team snaps. T. J. and John shared the rest. In order to throw, I would have to grab a guy after practice and ask nicely to put in a little work. Really, the only time I got to throw for any length of time was on Sundays before home games. I wouldn't dress for the game, but quarterbacks coach Karl Dorrell and I would work out before everyone came on to the field for their warm-ups. To complete the college analogy: 2012 felt like a redshirt year.

This was shaping up to be another time I'd be tempted to doubt what God had planned in front of me.

Waiting for your chance doesn't mean that you just sit around twiddling your thumbs. The opportunities you get in life come really fast, and you don't know when they'll arrive. I wasn't actually *playing*, but I was getting ready, and I was slowly improving in almost imperceptible ways. The proof? In 2013 I made the team—the *actual* team. I would be the third-string QB behind Schaub and Yates. I may have been a long way from starting, but I was headed in the right direction. And as they say in the NFL: You're always only a few plays away from getting a chance.

When that 2013 season got underway, an unexpected thing happened. Schaub struggled in a way that he never had before in his six years as the Texans' starter. A two-time Pro Bowler, he suddenly went on a cold streak. It definitely was not all his fault. Everyone was struggling, really, but Schaub was taking the brunt of the criticism. I felt bad. Matt had done a great job for the team, for the city of Houston. He is a great player, but for whatever reason, things were not going our way.

In Week 6, he injured his ankle against the Rams, and Yates got his chance. But then Yates—a guy who'd already won a playoff game in his young career—came in and threw a pick-six. We lost 38–13 and fell to 2–4.

The next day, Coach Kubiak asked to see me in his office. "Case, you're going to start on Sunday against the Chiefs," he said. My eyes were about as big as balloons—but I was ready. I had worked my tail off over the past year, and I was ready to play in a regular-season game.

I'll never forget standing in the tunnel before running onto the field in Kansas City that next Sunday. I specifically remember it because Kimberly and I had spoken earlier in the week about embracing the moment. I wanted to take special note of the sights, the sounds, and the feelings. This was a dream come true. I was about to take the field at Arrowhead, the loudest outdoor stadium in the world. *Holy crap.*

My first game didn't go down exactly how I imagined it might. It was ... *crazy.* The Chiefs were 6–0 at the time, and they had the league's stingiest defense. They were loaded with great players—Eric Berry, Tamba Hali, Derrick Johnson, Justin Houston, and Dontari Poe, to name a few. Our running back, Arian Foster, had to leave the game because of a back issue he suffered in the first series, and he didn't come back. (In fact, he didn't play again the rest of the season.) Then, in the second quarter, his backup, back Ben Tate, broke three ribs. He was out for a couple of series. So, when I completed a pass in the third quarter to tight end Garrett Graham, getting us down to the Chiefs' one-yard line, we didn't have any healthy backs to run our goal line plays. I actually remember turning around and handing the ball off to our fullback, Greg Jones, and thinking: *What the heck is going on?* We were a mess, and in the end we lost 17–16.

My next game was the complete opposite—it couldn't have started out better. I was having a blast at home against the Colts in a nationally-televised Sunday-nighter. Less than a minute in, Andre Johnson put a filthy double-move on Indy's Vontae Davis, a Pro Bowl-caliber corner. It was one of the easiest throws of my life—82-yard touchdown, up 7–0.

Later in the quarter I found Andre deep for 41 yards. Who said playing QB in the NFL was hard? I even got to show off my wheels with a 22-yard third-down run that set up another touchdown to Johnson. Not a bad half for Andre: 190 yards, 3 TDs. We were rolling; there was no way they'd stop us.

And then the unthinkable happened.

As we were trotting into the locker room for halftime, Gary Kubiak, a man who believed in me when no other head coach in the NFL did, suffered what's called a TIA or mini-stroke. Our entire team absolutely *loved* Coach Kubiak. Anyone who has ever played for a great coach at any level knows what I'm talking about—knows how much a coach can mean to his players. Kubes is one of those guys who you would try to run through a brick wall for. So when word started spreading around the locker room about the incident, we were shell-shocked. Defensive coordinator Wade Phillips came in and told us that Coach had passed out and was on the way to the hospital, and that he was stable. But that's all we got. As mentally tough as we all pretend to be, that proved too much for us. It was difficult to concentrate on football at that point. We stayed close, but our 55-yard field goal attempt sailed wide left as time expired. Altogether, it was a heartbreaking day.

There were a lot of moments to be proud of over the next six games—connecting with a promising young rookie named DeAndre Hopkins and hitting Andre for big plays; going toe-to-toe with Tom Brady in a 34–31 loss to the Patriots . . . But I also had some passes I'd like back.

The bottom line is: we lost all of them. Every game, except for one, finished within a touchdown—but we just couldn't pull everything together. This league is hard. *Really* hard. And there's no time to feel sorry for yourself after a loss, because there's always another team with a salty D that's ready to kick you while you're down the following

Sunday. And that's no fun. I wasn't used to the losing, and it knocked me off balance.

I fell into some bad habits. Instead of letting each game come to me, I tried to work my way out of the hole. I got up extra early to watch film, and I stayed up all night studying, thinking, trying to figure out how to get a win. I was pressing way too hard. And it wasn't right. It wasn't healthy. It wasn't *me*.

After a particularly tough loss at Jacksonville in Week 14, Texans owner Bob McNair fired Kubiak. I felt like I let my coach down. He was having a hard time with his health all season. Sometimes he was up in the booth, sometimes he was on the field. You could tell Coach wasn't himself. I remember I saw him at halftime of the loss to the Jaguars—his face looked so tired and just uncomfortable. As tough as it was at the time to see him get fired, I'm so grateful Coach Kubiak made it through that period OK and came out on the other side. He's a special person and his impact on my career has been huge.

During the loss streak, I was getting pretty down. One night I was holed up in the video room as usual, when I got a call from Tony Levine, my former coach at the University of Houston. Levine was actually head coach my final game because Sumlin had left for Texas A&M. He would then take over the job on a full-time basis the following season. But for most of the time I was there he coached special teams and receivers. Even though he didn't oversee my position, we got along really well. He would introduce me to recruits as the team's starting holder instead of starting quarterback. I loved Coach Levine's dry sense of humor and his coaching style. He was always able to put things into perspective.

"Case," he said, "I know you're down. Let me ask you a question. Are you a starting quarterback in the NFL?"

"Yeah."

"Is your wife at home?"

"Yeah."

"Does she still love you?"

"Yeah."

"So things aren't too bad, are they?"

"No, I guess not."

"Things are pretty good, aren't they?"

"Yeah, Coach, they sure are."

———

I had to do things the wrong way to get there, but I eventually learned some important lessons that year about how to prepare as a pro. That's me: I learn from my mistakes. I'm a grinder, and I have always counted on working hard to get where I want to be.

But after pouring myself out, week after week, physically and emotionally, I finally figured out that I needed something that would fill me up both emotionally and spiritually. I needed a daily quiet time in God's Word and in prayer. This is one of the ways to remain "in Christ."

Typically, I like to arrive at my team's facility early. And when I get there—after a cup or two of coffee—I get into the Word and I pray. I try to spend a quiet 10–20 minutes with God. This time is crucial for me. It resets me in my relationship with the Lord. It's essential to growing my faith. Even though I'm not a morning person, this has become a staple of every day. I know it's not in the commandments that you have a morning quiet time like this, but through the years people have encouraged me to do so. Beyond that, two examples from the Bible stand out:

> Very early in the morning, while it was still dark, [Jesus] got up, went out, and made his way to a deserted place; and there he was praying. —Mark 1:35

> In the morning, LORD, you hear my voice; in the morning I plead my case to you and watch expectantly. —Psalm 5:3

Jesus, the Son of God, and David, the king after God's own heart . . . two guys I think set a pretty good example to follow.

I know there are never enough hours in the day to do everything you want to do. But I'm glad God put only twenty-four hours in each day. If there were more, I would just try to fill them up with more . . . *stuff.* That's why I prioritize a quiet time in the morning.

If you're like me, then you care about what you do. And generally you spend a lot of your time on what you care about. There is no way we can spend all day reading the Bible and praying. But I believe that if you give God the firstfruits of your day, your mind tends to lean toward being Kingdom-minded from there on. And this is what being a Christian athlete is all about. I've said it before: I'm not a football player who happens to be a Christian. I'm a Christian who happens to play football. Christian athletes don't stop representing Jesus when we put our cleats on. Being a Christian isn't something you turn on and off. It's an *all-the-time* thing. And what if you're not an athlete? Just insert your job title and it still applies to you. Christian mom or dad, Christian businessman or teacher, Christian mailman, Christian chef . . .

Did I apply these lessons in my first year as a starter? Not all the time. Am I still working on living up to the standard that the Bible has set before us? Heck ya. But I believe that I planted important seeds in 2013. Now I was ready to head off and see: Where would I have the opportunity to grow next?

Chapter 11

Soaring on Eagles' Wings

To say that my first season as a starter with the Texans wasn't exactly what I had hoped for is putting it nicely. I had played good football at times that year, but I knew I needed to keep getting better, and I was ready to step up my game. On January 3, 2014, Houston hired former Patriots offensive assistant Bill O'Brien. He had coached Tom Brady in New England, so I was excited to learn from him. I quickly realized that O'Brien's offense was challenging. I was going to need to bring my A game. I felt good during that 2014 preseason even though I took primarily second-string snaps behind Ryan Fitzpatrick. I didn't necessarily play my best football, but I was getting the offense and was going to be able to help the team in whatever role they needed me to fill.

As the preseason came to an end, I felt that I was in pretty good shape. At that point of my career, there was always some doubt, but I wasn't too worried about being released. The Texans had their big cut day on a Friday following our final preseason game, and no phone call. *Phew* . . . in this business no news is good news. I headed into the weekend pretty relaxed. I went to see my Third Ward Coogs at their new stadium that Saturday, church with Kimberly on Sunday. Typical weekend . . . until the call.

It seems ironic that this call came while we were at church. A private number I didn't recognize that sent my stomach plummeting. I grabbed Kimberly's hand to make our escape from church because, well, I just knew. Sure enough, the voicemail confirmed it was *the person* I did not want to hear from: the "grim reaper."

Every team has a grim reaper; he's the employee in charge of rounding up the players who are about to be cut. I had been summoned to Coach O'Brien's office and I needed to bring my playbook.

If you're an NFL fan, you may have seen players getting cut by their coach on the HBO show *Hard Knocks*. And those guys aren't acting for the cameras—that's pretty much how it goes down. You walk into the coach's office and he breaks the bad news in a conversation that lasts a couple of minutes but feels like an eternity. I knew the Texans were going to release me once I got the call, so I drove to the facility feeling pretty bad. Bad, but not entirely hopeless. I wanted to face my destiny like a man. I also wanted to get some feedback from the coaches after they'd spent the offseason with me. I wanted to at least find out where I could improve and maybe even get some advice on taking the next steps as a player.

That's not what happened. Coach O'Brien looked right at me and told me I'd never be more than a third-string quarterback in the NFL. I knew I hadn't performed as well as I could that preseason, but I couldn't help but feel some anger. He went on to give some more specifics, but I didn't process much after that. Here I am coming off of a season in which I started eight games—some good games, some bad games—and now I was being told that I couldn't play at this level? I'm not sure if he was trying to motivate me or what, but it definitely got my competitive juices flowing. I knew this wasn't the end.

The NFL is funny. Everything comes at you fast, and you don't get a lot of time to figure things out. When you get released you have to wait twenty-four hours to clear waivers. But after that? I had no idea what was next. I just had to trust in the Lord.

That Sunday, Kimberly and I were invited to a neighbor's cookout. We were happy for the distraction as we waited to find out if anyone grabbed us on waivers, so we gladly accepted. We were having a nice time, actually. I mean, it's hard to be glum around a good barbecue, right? Still, I was having a little trouble being present, given the situation. *Was anyone going to pick me up? What happens if I clear waivers? What if no one wants me?* Three o'clock arrives and I'm doing my best to engage in the conversations around me, when my phone buzzes with a text from my buddy Zac: GO RAMS.

Go Rams? Zac is a Cowboys fan. Why was he texting me about the Rams? I immediately called him to ask, What's up? But before I could even do that, Kimberly got a text from a friend who'd taken a screenshot of *SportsCenter:* "Case Keenum picked up off waivers by the St. Louis Rams." *Wow! Is this real? The world found out before me that I was headed off to a new team?*

Just then my agent called and cleared up everything. St. Louis it was. Now, neither Kimberly nor I had ever lived outside of Texas; we thought one day we might have to because of my work, but we weren't exactly ready. We were definitely excited about that possibility. We just didn't have any time to mentally prepare for what had just been dropped on us. The season was starting in one week—less than a week actually—and I had to be in St. Louis *immediately*. I was on a plane by 7 p.m., leaving Kimberly to figure out how to transplant our entire life to another state. God knew I needed not just an incredible partner emotionally and spiritually, but the *best* logistical ninja there ever was. She handled this upheaval with complete grace and confidence (and again maybe a few tears), sending me on my way to focus on football while carrying the weight of this transition of her own. I could never have done any of this without her. *Never.*

It was daunting being away from our home state. Fortunately, we immediately met some great people in St. Louis. I quickly made close friends on the team and I felt extremely comfortable with the guys in the Rams' quarterback room. Sam Bradford, the starter, was both very talented and a great guy to be around. Shaun Hill, Sam's veteran backup, taught me so much about the mental aspect of the game. And Austin Davis, a third-year player out of Southern Miss—the man who beat me in that Conference USA title game way back in 2011—became a close friend.

It was a totally different environment. We were focused on football, but we also hung out. When we needed a break from watching video, our game of choice was Spades. We were all pretty competitive dudes and had some epic card games. I was starting to learn a different approach to preparation: Do all your work, but don't forget to have a life and have some fun.

The one thing that wasn't happening for me in St. Louis was getting on the field. I was third-string and eventually demoted to the practice squad so the team could get more help on special teams. During this time, I held on closely to Isaiah 40:31. "They who wait on the LORD shall renew their strength" (ESV). The Hebrew word that this Bible verse was originally written in is *qavah* (ka-VAH'), meaning to wait, look eagerly for, lie in wait for, or linger for. I imagine this waiting like a waiter at a restaurant. When you have a really good waiter, your iced tea is always filled. The chips and the queso are *flowing*. (I'm a Mexican food fanatic.) That server is really good at what he does because he enjoys it. He loves to do it. And in a way, he's loving the ones he's serving so well.

Just like a waiter eagerly looking for every opportunity to delight his table, I want to be found waiting on God's unfailing love and guidance. And because of the love He has for me, I long to serve Him with faith and joy right where He's placed me.

Now, that's not to say there weren't humbling moments. One time, when I was with the Rams, I was sitting around in the training room before a spring practice when one of the rookies approached me.

"Hey," he said. "Is this where we can get our ankles taped?"

"It sure is, bud," I replied.

"Can you tape my ankles?"

I thought he was joking or maybe someone was pulling a prank and had put him up to it. Man, one of the other QBs got me good. And this kid was a good actor.

Then it hit me. *He thinks I'm an athletic trainer.*

Well, I got him back. That had to be one of the worst tape jobs any NFL player has ever gotten.

I am not a status guy. I don't brag about myself and I always aspire to put others first. I fit in most crowds and if you didn't know who I was, you probably wouldn't think I'm an NFL quarterback. But wearing that uniform does give me opportunities. God sure has shown favor and increased my platform. My prayer and goal in life is to stay committed to making His name known. Athletes have a voice. And like so many other players in the league, I want to make a difference. Most importantly, I want to give Him all the glory.

———

To me, serving is making a difference in some way, helping someone else along, or being a better person myself. I stay open to His love and guidance at all times, not because it's a burden or something that I have to do, but out of pure joy. I'm not simply twiddling my thumbs, waiting on the Lord. I'm actively looking to see where I can serve and be a better person. Waiting on the Lord means being ready when He puts an opportunity in front of my face. Coach Gruden's words from our *QB Camp* meeting, before I entered the league, still echoed in my head: "Just be ready, just be ready, just be ready."

Week after week passed that year, and I kept waiting for God to show me where I could serve, but before I knew it the season was about to end. I was already thinking ahead to the offseason, when I knew there would be some unknowns. I was eager to find out what plans God had for me next. We got to Week 14, a Thursday night game for us, and afterward our coach, Jeff Fisher, gave us the weekend off. For me, that meant an opportunity to recharge and have some fun.

Northern Missouri offers some incredible whitetail deer hunting. They're huge up there, compared to the ones I'd become familiar with growing up in Texas. I mean we have some big deer with some really nice antler spreads back home, but the cold weather up in Missouri bred some *big* bodied deer. And this Texas boy was enjoying a new type of hunting I had never experienced before. I'd befriended a couple of teammates, and we knew a man who had a great little piece of property that was perfect for hunting. That

Sunday evening I decided to bring my climber tree stand out into the woods and see what walked by.

There I was, sitting in my stand with my bow, overlooking a beautiful river and a gorgeous stretch of hardwoods. There was an un-harvested soybean field in front of me and I had a good feeling that I was going to bag a 12-point monster.

In the end, I got way more than I could have asked for.

After watching the squirrels for a while, I did what most bored hunters do in their deer blind. I took my phone out. The first thing I noticed was that my wife had texted me. Kimberly had been watching my old team, the Texans, on TV and she told me that their quarterback, Ryan Fitzpatrick, had been injured. That was not good news; Ryan had become a close friend of mine. But before I could even respond, she texted me another piece of news: Ryan's backup, Tom Savage, a rookie out of Rutgers, was limping around. Shane Lechler, a veteran *punter* who hadn't played quarterback since college, was throwing passes on the sideline, warming up. (Look it up: Lechler is in the Texas High School Hall of Fame as a quarterback. That dude is a baller.) *What is happening down there?* I wondered.

So I'm starting to lose focus on getting that prize deer, and I'm starting to think about football. Since I was only on the Rams' practice squad, any team in the league could sign me to its active roster. Now, we missed our friends and family for sure. But it's not like we'd been praying to go back to Houston. Being part of the Rams felt right all season long.

As usual, though, God had different plans for me. An hour later, I'm still in the deer stand and my agent calls. "The Texans want to sign you *right now*," he said. "Oh, and, by the way: You're probably going to start next week against the Baltimore Ravens." My heart started *pounding*. It was dead quiet out there in those woods, but I'm pretty sure you could hear my heart thumping from a mile away. Looking back, I'm pretty sure my prized whitetail deer walked right under the tree I was sitting in without me even noticing.

Starting in Houston again sure sounded like an amazing opportunity, but there was doubt in my mind. For one, I knew Coach O'Brien didn't believe in me. I wasn't sure I wanted to play for a team that didn't appreciate what I brought to the table. *What's the right decision? Can I go back to Houston? Will it be different this time?*

Text messages are flying now. I'm calling my agents, family, close friends. We're all trying to figure this out and do the right thing. Then, for just a moment, my phone goes quiet and I'm alone up there on the deer stand.

Far from Houston. Far from Kimberly. Far from my family.

I'm staring out at this majestic countryside, lost in my head, when I look down the river bend and see this odd shape emerge. I look closer and it was a big black bird with a white head and white tail, soaring majestically. Boy, it seemed like it was gliding forever. It followed the path of the river and then went into the trees, only to reemerge and come back the other way up the river. Is that ... *a bald eagle?*

I had never seen a bald eagle in person before, but I was certain that this was one. (Later on, the friend who owned the property confirmed that bald eagles had indeed been spotted in the area over the years.) I immediately made the connection to Isaiah 40:31: "But they who trust in the LORD will renew their strength; they will soar on wings like eagles; they will run and not become weary; they will walk and not faint." It had to be a sign. *Yes! Let's go back to Houston and do this thing!*

Only this time I was going to be different. Even though I wasn't on the field, I grew a lot in St. Louis. I'd spent my first stint with the Texans being really tough on myself. When things didn't go well, I would just hit my head against the wall repeatedly trying to figure out the problem. This time, it helped that I didn't have any time to overthink things. I was going to start a game in less than a week!

My stats in that start against Baltimore—20 of 42, 185 yards, one interception, and zero touchdowns—weren't going to blow anyone away. Running back Arian Foster was actually the star passer; he threw a touchdown on a trick play in the red zone. But I was able to make enough plays to help my new team win 25–13. Afterward, words from a fellow native Abilenian rang true. Major league pitcher and World Series champ John Lackey, one of our town's biggest sources of pride, texted me, "All those tough times are what makes winning feel so darn good." And John was so right. Losing eight games the previous season was awful. But all the work I'd put into getting better, all the tough times—that made the win so much more special. I don't know how many people will remember a Week 15 win over the Ravens, but it felt better than darn good.

The next week, I was careful not to fall into some of the old habits from our eight-game losing streak. I wasn't going to over-prepare and get caught up in negative thinking. If Coach O'Brien was going to cuss me out in practice, I wasn't going to let it get to me. I had a ton of studying to do to catch up on the playbook, but I wasn't going to stay at the facility late into the evenings. I was going to make sure I spent time with Kimberly. I was way behind on prep, but our Friday date night was a priority.

In Week 17 we faced the Jacksonville Jaguars at home. There was an outside possibility that we could reach the playoffs, so the stakes were high. The game started off well: I threw a 10-yard touchdown to Foster on our first drive, and we jumped out to a 7–0 lead. Jacksonville hit a field goal—7–3—but the next time we had the ball we were driving again. Then I made a mistake. Cornerback Dwayne Gratz stepped in front of a pass intended for DeAndre Hopkins and returned it 55 yards for a touchdown to give the Jags a 10–7 lead.

Twelve months earlier, a pick-six would have sent me into a tailspin. Not this year. I came back out firing, and we took back the lead, 14–10, on the very next drive. I finished the day with 250 yards and two touchdowns. More importantly, we won 23–17.

Unfortunately, the Ravens beat the Browns that same afternoon, knocking us out of the playoffs, but I still felt pretty proud that I could help the Texans win two games. Coach O'Brien told me I was a different dude than the guy he'd cut five months earlier. He even said we'd talk about our meeting back in August, and while that conversation still hasn't happened, that's OK with me. I learned a lot of ball from him, and what he said motivated me big time. God puts people in your life for the exact right reason at the exact right time.

I probably would've signed back with the Texans that year even if I hadn't seen that bald eagle, but I'm still glad God gave me that sign. It reminded me how much bigger His plans are for us than our own. That 2014 season had its ups and downs, as seasons in life all do. The difference this year was that I could soar, just like the eagle that so clearly revealed to me the presence of God those weeks prior. I knew in a deeper way that my life and my purpose in football is so much bigger than circumstances or mistakes. God so evidently orchestrated my journey to this point, and I knew now that no matter what happened, He was good and would never let me down.

Chapter 12

Go Rams

G oing into that offseason I had no idea what the future held in Houston, but I was feeling a new sense of confidence after winning my first two NFL games. I didn't know where my next home would be, but my agents predicted I would probably sign another one-year deal with the Texans—but then the offseason took on a life of its own, as I've learned it tends to do.

The Cleveland Browns released quarterback Brian Hoyer, who had played for Coach O'Brien in New England. And I knew what that might mean. My agents told me to just hold on and see what happens, but I didn't have to hold on long. On March 11, 2015, my agents called back to inform me that the Texans had traded me to the St. Louis Rams for a 2016 seventh-round pick. I guess I wasn't going to get a chance to build on those two wins. Still, I wasn't too down on myself. I had enjoyed St. Louis and the friendships I developed a year earlier.

Not long after I got the news, I turned on ESPN to see what was happening, and I saw on the ticker: "Rams trade for QB." *Yes!* Now I was pumped. *Here we go!* Then the next sentence scrolled across: "Rams acquire quarterback Nick Foles from Philadelphia Eagles." *Ohhh ... I thought they were talking about me. I guess the Rams traded for two QBs.*

Unfortunately, the news of my trade was blasted out to the world before I could tell my family. This has happened with virtually every key move throughout my entire pro career. I was leaving Texas. I was a bit nervous about the trade at first, but that's when Coach Jeff Fisher gave me a call.

Fisher said, "Let's go."

"Yes! Let's go, Coach!"

It felt really good to have a team want me. They even gave up a draft pick to get me. I know it was only a seventh-rounder, but to an undrafted guy, it still felt pretty good.

I loved playing for Coach Fisher. He gets a bad rap sometimes because the quarterbacks he had with the Rams found success only later on in their career for other coaches—Foles, Jared Goff, and myself. But Fisher believed in his players and fostered a great atmosphere to play in. He's a true players' coach. I still remember some early morning film sessions when he would stop by and bring his old hunting dog to keep me company while I studied opponents' defenses.

A fresh start in St. Louis was just what I needed to keep the momentum going from the previous season. Nick and I became fast friends. We were both believers, both from Texas, and both married to our best friend. We tend to see the world through the same lens. I came in that season to be the backup; my job was to support Nick. I'm always in favor of a quarterback room with defined roles. It makes life a bit less stressful for everyone.

I know there is always a little drama with the quarter-back position. And there is always going to be competition. That's what makes playing the position so great. There's only one football and only one guy can play at a time. If you're a wide receiver then two, three, maybe four can be on the field at once, and almost every position has guys rotate in. Not at QB, though; that's the one position to which everyone looks to set the tone for the team.

On the field that summer I started to apply some of the lessons I had learned in my previous seasons. I wasn't a rookie anymore, and it was really nice to be over that hump. The preseason went well. I was OK with being the backup . . . but, once again, the plans I'd made were quite different from what the Lord had in mind for me.

Sometimes, even when you have good people in place, teams still struggle. The personnel don't click. Chemistry doesn't form. That's football. That's the NFL. We started out OK in 2015, jumping out to a 4–3 start. But then our offense hit a wall. After a 37–13 loss to the Bears in Week 10, Fisher decided to make a change.

We were sitting in the quarterbacks room that Monday when Coach Fisher walked in. "I'm going with Case," he said to us. Nick and I asked everyone else to leave so we could talk, and we had a great conversation. I believe that you learn a lot about the people in your life when things get tough. When you're down, look around and see who's there. You know those are your *true* friends; those are your boys who have your back. And Nick is one of those guys—a great football player and an even better person. I'll ride with him any day. Even if he did go on to beat me in the 2018 NFC Championship Game.

I have to admit, though, I was a little surprised by Coach Fisher's decision. I knew I could start in the NFL, but I had come into the season accepting that I'd be on the bench, that I'd be ready in case of an injury. But I also shouldn't be surprised by anything that happens in this league. Opportunities don't come around very often. And as I've said before, just being ready was always on my mind.

Now, I didn't have much time to think about it. The Baltimore Ravens were coming up the following Sunday. I had beaten them the year before with the Texans, but I knew their defense was always raring to go.

That game was a *battle*. After 58 minutes, the score was deadlocked at 13. After they missed a field goal attempt with 1:13 left, we got the ball back with a chance to win it. On the second play of the drive, we were able to draw them offside. The refs didn't blow the play dead, though, so it was a free play. I figured we'd try the old Aaron Rodgers move: run around a little and throw the ball downfield. But I should have just spiked the ball or thrown it away. Linebacker Elvis Dumervil got off to a fast start and was on top of me immediately, and when he sacked me my head snapped back, bouncing against the turf . . . *hard*.

One of the reasons it's so difficult to treat concussions is that every one of them is different. This was a hard hit and I immediately brought my hands up to my head. When I tried to get up, I felt dizzy. I stumbled a bit when my lineman Garrett Reynolds tried to help me up. Trainer Reggie Scott ran on to the field. The Rams have a great training staff— wonderful people who are truly committed to helping the guys on the team.

"Case, are you OK?" Reggie asked me.

"Yeah, I'm OK. Should I stay down?" I responded.

"Yeah, get down."

Just then, the nearest official turned toward us and saw Reggie. "What the ---- are you doing on the field?" the official yelled. "Get out of here."

Reggie asked me again if I was all right and I said, "Yes." And I meant it. My legs came back underneath me and my head cleared up. Before I had time to really think about what was going on, the play call started coming into my helmet from the offensive coordinator. Reggie cleared out and we got back to work.

On the next play I threw a short pass to Wes Welker that was barely out of his grasp. But we still had a chance. I dropped back again and—this time I didn't see linebacker Courtney Upshaw. I was looking downfield and he came around my backside and poked the ball out of my hand. Baltimore recovered and one minute later they hit the game-winning field goal. *Totally* my fault. That was a tough way to end the game, compounded by what happened in the coming hours and days.

I was down on myself after the loss. I was also trying to figure out exactly what was going on with my body. I experienced fatigue and headaches. I'm not sure if I was tired from working so hard all week or if it was the blow to my head. Sure, I had a headache, but maybe it was from everyone I know texting me to *ask me* if I had a headache. If people ask a thousand times a day whether you have a headache, believe me: then you have a headache.

The Rams did the right thing and put me in the concussion protocol. But the fact that I had remained in the game after hitting the turf so hard became a national story. The NFL is still trying to figure out how to manage the concussion problem. It's not easy in the flow of the moment. As a competitor, it's hard to take yourself out of the game. My name was in the headlines all week, and not for the reasons I wanted. I had a great rapport with the training staff. Reggie and the guys treat everyone with respect, and the players' health is their No. 1 priority. They caught some flak from the media, though, for how they handled the situation. They shouldn't have. Reggie was on the field that day because he was looking after me.

In the past, the concussion and the subsequent controversy would have been another reason to get down on myself, something to knock me off balance and prevent me from being the best player I can be. But my experience in the league and my continued spiritual growth had me well prepared for anything coming my way. The entire ordeal also served as an important reminder: Our window to play football at this level is limited. I have so much respect for anyone who has played the sport professionally. Sometimes I work out with retired players and they have trouble moving around. You know it just by watching them. They gave up their bodies for their career. I know there's a risk. But at least we're taking the risk. Anyone who has ever taken a chance on something they care about and failed should still feel proud about taking their shot. Without risk, there's nothing to gain.

I'm constantly reminded that players have to take advantage of every opportunity. I had to sit out the next game because I was in the concussion protocol. But it wasn't long before I felt much better, and I couldn't wait to get back on the field. The coaching staff decided to give me another shot against the Lions in Week 14. I did a lot of handing off to Todd Gurley that day, but that was just fine with me, because we won 21–14 to break our five-game losing streak.

The following week we got to open up the offense just a little more. I didn't throw much, but when I did I connected. I hit Kenny Britt for a 60-yard TD and Tavon Austin for a 17-yard score. My final line: 14-of-17, 234 yards, two touchdowns. We won 31–23.

All right, getting a little streak going.

Next up: "The Legion of Boom," the Seattle Seahawks, at one of the loudest outdoor stadiums, CenturyLink Field. There's nothing like going against the best to bring out your best. I threw a 28-yard touchdown to Kenny Britt just past the outstretched arms of Pro Bowler Richard Sherman, and we won 23–17.

Three in a row.

Could we make it four in a row to close out the season?

It wasn't mean to be. We missed a field-goal attempt in the closing seconds of regulation against the 49ers and lost 19–16 in overtime. But the blueprint for success had been laid out in the final month of that season. I remember walking off the field after Week 17 bummed that we didn't win that day, but also thinking, *We can do something with this squad.*

———

Our time in St. Louis went by quickly. Partly because Kimberly and I were in and out, in and out, but mostly because of the great relationships we formed off the field. Offensive lineman Barrett Jones and tight end Brad Smelley, my best friends from the team, lived down the hall from us. It sure made our tiny apartment building in St. Charles feel like a bona fide college dorm. Our friendship grew quickly over late-night *FIFA* throw-downs, board game battles, and never-ending games of Spades. (Kimberly and I still hold the winning record.)

Our second season in St. Louis proved to be one of the most important times in our spiritual lives because of two wonderful people we were introduced to by Barrett: Jon and Tracy Sullivan. Jon and Tracy were friends with Barrett from his hometown of Memphis, and Barrett had spent plenty of time at their home, meeting with Jon for discipleship. Barrett asked if I wanted to join the group and be discipled by Jon as well. I had very little idea of what this meant, but I was definitely in a place where I knew I wanted my spiritual walk to grow deeper. This seemed like a good start.

If you have no idea what it means to "disciple," don't worry; I didn't either. Let me give you some insight:

In the Bible when Jesus started His ministry, He found twelve dudes—His twelve bros that would be with Him until the end, His disciples. These twelve men would be by His side for three years of ministry work. Jesus performed miracles, preached sermons, and lived His life alongside these guys in such a way that they would become like Him. Jesus was a mentor, and He built His followers to be disciple-makers who would multiply themselves by turning others into lifelong learners and followers of Jesus too. Jesus' strategy and their way of life comes into focus in His last command to them.

His final instructions appear in the Bible at the end of Matthew, one of His disciples' account:

Then Jesus came near and said to them, "All authority has been given to me in heaven and on earth. Go, therefore, and make disciples of all nations, baptizing them in the name of the Father and of the Son and of the Holy Spirit, teaching them to observe everything I have commanded you. And remember, I am with you always, to the end of the age." —Matthew 28:18–20

This is commonly referred to as the Great Commission. The last command that He gives us, as His followers, in His Word today. I learned from Jon that the first word *go* is more specifically translated from the original Greek as "as you are going" or "having gone." In other words, the command from Jesus isn't simply to go somewhere; it's to make disciples wherever you are—as you are going. This small lesson blew me away. If you've ever had the experience of God's Word coming alive for the first time, then you understand what I mean. A seemingly simple Scripture that I've read many times before suddenly hit me in a powerful new way.

This command that Jesus was giving to His disciples was not just for them, but for all people who follow Christ. In my mind, what once sounded like, "Pastors, go and make disciples. Chaplains, go and make disciples. Ministers, go and make disciples," I now understood to be, "*Everyone*, as you are going, make disciples of all people." Whether you're a football player, teacher, coach, businessman, scientist, engineer, or pilot . . . you are there to make disciples.

Jon met with Barrett, Brad, and me every week to talk through the Bible and what it looks like to make disciples in our own lives, and Kimberly did the same with Tracy and a small group of women. Jon and Tracy modeled how to make intentional investments into the lives of others by following Jesus' strategy, inviting us to walk alongside them and opening their home and family to us, sharing with us "not only the gospel of God but also [their] own lives" (1 Thessalonians 2:8).

After the season ended, our time together culminated with my first ever mission trip to South Africa. Our group had grown to be more than friends. Brad, Barrett, Tracy, Jon—these people were our St. Louis family. As Kimberly and I traveled with them to the poorer areas outside of Johannesburg and Mokopane, no one cared that we were professional football players. It wasn't even worth explaining that I held the all-time college football passing record. I realized that, frankly, those things really didn't matter. What mattered to them was not my accomplishments or my accolades—it was my heart. It mattered that I was there, in their world, loving, teaching, playing, and praying with them.

We were so impacted by the joy they carried through what appeared to us as so much hardship. This was exactly where I needed to be. I was just a *person*, just like them. They had dreams and passions and ambitions. They had needs and struggles, just like me. And just like me, they needed a Savior. They were hungry to learn more about Jesus and His message of salvation. It was a blatant reminder that I was put on this planet for more than football. My highest calling is to serve Jesus Christ and love His flock. I will lay down my life any day to do this, however He asks.

Everything seemed to be falling into place in St. Louis. I had great relationships with my teammates and my coaches. I was growing in my spiritual life and picking up friends and mentors. I wanted to see where all of this positive momentum would take me and the Rams.

As it turns out, that would be a long, long way away from St. Louis.

Chapter 13

Goin' Hollywood

The first day *Hard Knocks* cameras showed up at my house, I didn't quite know what to make of them. I consider myself to be a pretty genuine guy, but having a camera in your face all day feels a little overwhelming. It's not the easiest thing to have a normal conversation with a boom mic hovering over your head. I was glad to discover that the NFL Films crew was incredibly professional and began to feel like friends immediately as they started to film our lives. They told us, "Just go about your business." Umm, what business? We just moved to L.A. with the rest of the team.

"Do you want me to just sit on the couch and watch *The Office*? This is what we'd normally do at 8 o'clock." (The irony of watching *The Office* while feeling like we were on *The Office*...)

Luckily, the producers asked Kimberly and me a few questions to get us going, and America got a glimpse inside the L.A. version of the Keenum household.

A lot of NFL players I know watch *Hard Knocks* every August. I've always found the show interesting. Just like football fans everywhere, I get caught up in who will and won't make the team, what coach is cussing out his players, and what kind of drama is going to unfold during such a crucial time for players. Never really thought I'd be part of it, but it added to what was quite a surreal time on the West Coast.

You see, in January, the owners approved the Rams' move from St. Louis to Los Angeles. The franchise was originally based in L.A. but had moved to St. Louis in 1994. Now we were all headed West and didn't have much time to make it happen. On top of that, the Rams were chosen to be the featured team on *Hard Knocks* that offseason.

Kimberly got to show off her football IQ by going over plays with me. My favorite shots from the show were when Kimberly was in the kitchen making waffles while helping me study. She would be mixing up the batter, pause, and call out a play: "West Right Slot 2-Jet X Dagger, Y Shallow Cross." Then I would visualize my play and talk through my reads. And we repeated that process for most of my practice scripts. I told you, her football knowledge is legit. She was incredible.

We got to go on Ryan Seacrest's radio program together, and Kimberly made him and his entire staff her "victory waffles." Ryan asked what the key ingredient was . . . Kimberly said "a lot of butter" . . . I chimed in with "a lot of love."

It was all fun, but nothing we were used to. L.A. is just a *little* different than back home. On the main strip in Abilene, Buffalo Gap Road, the stoplights start flashing at 8 p.m. It doesn't matter, because there are hardly even cars on the road. In comparison, it once took me over three hours to get from Thousand Oaks, where we lived, to training camp at UC Irvine. But Kimberly and I adjusted the best we could. It didn't take long before I was going to brunch and ordering avocado toast and acai bowls.

I'm not sure people realize how much work goes into displacing an entire franchise. Usually when you arrive with a new team, they are able to help ease the players and their families' transition. They can help you with little things, like finding a good doctor for your wife and kids or telling you where you can get a tune-up for your car. Everybody on the Rams was flying blind. We were all trying to figure things out together and we didn't have a lot of time. I still remember Googling how to get to my facility in Week 1. Pretty sure I was the only starting QB in the NFL who didn't know how to drive to work.

After the 2015 season, I started reading stories about a potential relocation. When the staff came in and started labeling everything and doing a full inventory, that was a good clue we were on the go. But we still weren't sure, and nobody was saying if we were moving. What I didn't expect that offseason was a blockbuster trade to move up in the draft. On April 14, the Rams sent the No. 15 overall pick, two second-round picks, a third-round pick, and the following season's first- and third-rounders to the Tennessee Titans for the No. 1 pick.

When I won three out of my last four games the previous season, I thought that I had a chance to make my time with the Rams a long-term situation. All my postseason meetings went well. Offensive coordinator Rob Boras was returning. We had continuity and I felt we were poised to make a move in the NFC West. But I also knew that if they were going all the way up there to No. 1, that had to be for a quarterback.

Sure enough, the Rams selected University of California quarterback Jared Goff with the first pick. I have to admit, it wasn't easy watching skill position players fly off the board that the team wasn't drafting because they didn't have their picks anymore. At this point, however, I knew the game. It turns out Goff was a great guy and we had a cohesive quarterback room. I just wasn't ready to let go of the starting job.

When we found out about the move to L.A, we were concerned about losing our connection to the spiritual community we formed in St. Louis. We had just met Jon and Tracy and they were teaching both Kimberly and me so much. But I was reminded in Los Angeles that discipleship isn't just for pastors and deacons. Whatever you're doing, you have the chance to make disciples.

We were starting from scratch in California, but we knew we had an amazing opportunity to thrive right where God placed us. As we continued to get filled up with the knowledge of God's love, we were able to take that precious understanding and pass it on to those around us. It wasn't easy, starting over in a huge city that was so foreign to us, but you should have seen my wife. Kimberly is an all-star. She worked so hard to gather the players' wives and girlfriends for get-togethers and Bible studies and poured her life out day after day to love them through this wild transition. Her discipleship and care for these women was instrumental in the team dynamic and unity.

All in all, our team really came together because of this move. Normally, when a player switches teams, they are transplanted and dropped into a whole new world. They, along with their families, have to find new friends, homes, restaurants, new everything. With this entire team move, everyone was figuring it out. It's nice when you have about fifty buddies who are clueless right alongside you. Doing all this together made the year that much more special because of the bonds we formed with teammates and their families.

The actual business of football got off to exactly the kind of start we didn't want. We lost to the 49ers 28–0 in our season-opener. I know that score sounds terrible, and it was, but I could tell that we weren't that far off. I had to fall back on some old lessons.

"I think I was seeing ghosts," I said in a press conference later that week. "I was seeing things that weren't there. I wasn't trusting myself and my abilities."

Trust.

That loss would have gotten me really down earlier in my career. We had our first game in our new Los Angeles home the following Sunday and I needed to have my head in the right place. I didn't have time to focus on the ghosts . . . we faced the Seahawks on Sunday, and the "Legion of Boom," unlike my ghosts, was very much real.

In the past, I might have come out that week trying to be perfect and overthink every aspect of the game. Once again, I had to make myself leave the building on Friday early.

Don't watch any more film. Relax and rest for the game.

Sunday rolled around and I was in a good place. When I got the opportunity to run out of the tunnel into the Coliseum as the first Rams quarterback to start a game in

L.A. in twenty years, I was pumped. As far as the fans, well, let's just say it wasn't Texas.

In our first home game we were up 9–3 over the Seahawks. Not quite a barnburner, I know. But late in the game we needed to convert a third down to seal the win. I look up in the stands, and everyone is doing the Wave. Not exactly locked in on what's happening on the field . . . that's L.A. for you. They love the Rams, but they never lose sight of the entertainment factor.

We clinched that victory, and then followed it up with road wins over Tampa Bay and Arizona to improve to 3–1. The Rams hadn't started out 3–1 in a long time. But our early success was never the narrative. Neither was playing in L.A. Those were just subplots to the one story the media seemed most interested in: Everywhere I turned, I heard, *"When are the Rams going to put in Jared Goff?"* I didn't mind in training camp. All the cameras were focused on the No. 1 pick, so I could work on my game without any distractions.

When we won three out of the first four, the Goff storyline didn't bother me either. Jared couldn't have been cooler, and I could see he was trying to figure everything out like any rookie. He was working to get better each week just like me.

For whatever reason, we just couldn't keep our early momentum as a team going. We had talent, but we began finding ways to lose.

In Week 6, we fell to the Bills at the Coliseum. I remember telling Kimberly after each of those losses that I thought I had played really well. I just wanted two-to-three passes back. That's what is so hard about this league. The difference between winning ten games and making the playoffs, and winning four and having your head coach getting fired, comes down to a handful of plays—maybe ten over the course of the entire season. It truly is a game of inches. I think that's why the NFL is so popular. Where else can you find that kind of drama week in and week out? I love it ... when we win.

Week 7 we went to Detroit and I had one of my best games as a pro: 27-for-32, 321 yards, three passing TDs, one running TD. I actually completed 21 straight passes at one point. It didn't matter. Another Texas QB, Matthew Stafford, was just a little better and the Lions beat us 31–28.

I admit; I had to shut off my phone at a certain point. I generally stay off social media during the season. Seems like no matter how good things are, there is always somebody that wants to give their nasty opinion. I was getting a little tired of people asking about how I was doing with Goff looking over my shoulder. Thinking about that wasn't going to help me be of service to the team.

We traveled to London to face the Giants in Week 9, and the ball just didn't bounce our way all afternoon. Either I would barely overthrow my target or a receiver would slip on the Twickenham Stadium turf. In the game of inches, we were just an inch off every time. But we still fought hard and were in it 'til the very end. Trailing 17–10, we drove deep into Giants territory in the final minute and I threw my fourth and final pick. *Not a fun day.*

That was a long trip home from England, but the following week we beat the Jets 9–6 to improve to 4–5. Not the prettiest win, but once again, we played hard and were happy with the outcome. And I thought we were still in the playoff picture. At 4–5, you're very much in it. Turns out the Green Bay Packers were 4–5 as well, and they went on to make the postseason. I never thought for a second that we weren't in the mix. Maybe that's why I didn't see what was about to happen next.

Ironically, the meeting went down exactly the same way as when Coach Fisher came in and told me I would be taking over for Foles the season before. Déjà vu. He came into the meeting room where Jared and I were watching film and told us that Jared would be starting against the Dolphins in Week 11. "I'm going with Jared," Coach Fisher said matter-of-factly. Just like with me and Nick, Jared and I had a great talk afterward. I didn't agree with the coaching staff's decision.

But I have come to understand the business of professional football.

We didn't win another game that year. People ask me if that felt like a wasted season. I don't view it that way at all. The experts at different media outlets had all sorts of opinions, I'm sure. Anyone on the outside looking in would probably think that it was really bad. And a lot of that year was tough for sure. Losing sucks. It's a production business, and when you aren't producing, it's tough to stick around. Nevertheless, I'm proud of the way I played for the Rams. We were a young team who played hard and managed to win some games. I was voted team captain by the team and wore the "C" on my jersey with pride. A lot of good memories with some high-quality people. Would I change some things? Sure. But looking back, the whole time, God was doing some cool things behind the scenes.

I didn't know what was going to happen after the season. I could tell you what I had planned, but as you might have guessed, God has His own designs . . . and they were better than what I could have even imagined.

Chapter 14

Minnesota Nice

B orn and raised in Texas, I didn't really know what I was in for with the weather in Minnesota. I mean, it can't be that bad, right? When I signed there in the spring and worked out in the summer, we loved it. The hottest summer months were mild to us Texans, and the sun stayed out later to make the days extra long. In July, it stayed light enough for me to play golf or stay out on the lake up until 10 p.m. I could get used to this. The fall? That's a different story.

The first time it snowed, I was in trouble. I found a rather flimsy plastic snow shovel in the garage of our rental house in Edina, Minnesota. I thought, *I'm a professional athlete. I'm from Texas. I should be able to shovel snow.* I get out there in the driveway and I'm baffled. *Do you put the rock salt down before you shovel or after?* I had waited a day or two after the snow fell and had driven over it a few times in the drive-way before I even attempted this project. I was making all the rookie mistakes. I didn't even know where the snow was supposed to go. It doesn't melt? It doesn't melt. *It never melts.*

I'm out there basically trying to figure out which end of the shovel to hold when a neighbor drove by and yelled, "Case, what are you doing?"

"I honestly have no idea, man," I said.

"You're going to hurt yourself if you do it like that," he said. "Just stop. We'll take care of it."

"We do have a game this week, it wouldn't look good if I showed up on the injury report because of a shoveling incident."

After that night I never saw snow on my driveway. I mean never. I had neighbors on either side who were competing to wake up earlier to shovel. They were great. They call it "Minnesota Nice" up there. To me, it's a *literal* example of the biblical command to "love thy neighbor." The people reminded me a lot of folks back home in Abilene.

I came in to Minnesota to back up Sam Bradford, my former Rams teammate. Third-year player Teddy Bridgewater was also on the team, working on rehabbing a serious knee injury he suffered in 2016. We had a solid QB room. I really enjoyed being with those guys all year. Coach Kevin Stefanski kept us in line but each of us learned a lot from one another. Teddy, whose bright career start was threatened by the injury, would always remind me to "smile, have fun, man," when the moment got too tense. Great advice. We were about to have a lot of fun that season.

Bradford had one of the best games of his career in Week 1. He was 27-for-32 for 346 yards and a touchdown in a win over the Saints. I mean, *he was on*. Spinning it, dropping dimes, absolutely in the zone. But he hurt his knee on a play early in the game. Back in St. Louis, Bradford repeatedly had knee trouble. The coaches told me to be ready just in case.

As the week went on, we weren't getting any definitive answers. Sam and I were splitting the reps and they just didn't know if he was going to be able to go. On Friday, Bradford took a higher percentage of the reps, so I figured he would play against the Steelers on the road.

I arrived at the stadium on Sunday still not knowing for sure either way. Pittsburgh is a tough place to go play under the best of circumstances. This was going to be tough for either Sam or me. I was in the locker room when Stefanski walked in. "Alright, you're up," he said. Just like that, I was starting my first game for the Vikings. I felt ready, but sometimes games don't work out. We lost to the Steelers 26–9 and I failed to throw a touchdown.

Not the start you want.

The next week, some familiar feelings crept back in. I knew I needed to have a big game the following week. I was still getting to know the team around me . . . and they were getting to know me. In the past, I would have really pressed—staying up all hours studying, worrying about how I'm going to play. I like to think I've learned a lot in that regard, but I'm not going to lie: I was anxious to do well. That's who I am. I love to compete and I'm going to try to help the team win any way I can.

At this point of my career, I had learned I can't get lost in that. If I sound like a broken record, that's because I'm hardheaded and stubborn. I seem to be circling back to the same lessons God has taught me before. I came back to the essential truth that had guided me since I was in high school—I'm playing for the audience of One. I'm giving it my all out there every day in practice and on game day for one reason—to glorify God. I kept circling one word in my head: *Trust. Trust* myself, *trust* my teammates, *trust* my coaches, *trust* the play, *trust* my training and preparation. Most importantly, *trust* God. I made this my mind-set for the week and gradually it became my mind-set for the year.

Trust beyond what you can see. That's faith.

The following week we faced the Tampa Buccaneers, a team I had beaten the last two seasons. From the get-go, I was able to put the frustration I felt the week before behind me. We came out and hit them hard. I connected with Adam Thielen for a 45-yard bomb on the first play from scrimmage.

Pat Shurmur and I had gone over the first 15 plays together and this one had me really excited. It was a great protection . . . we slide the entire offensive line strong and let the back take the backside defensive end. Well, they brought a pressure to the strong side, the same way the line was sliding and dropped the defensive end the halfback had to block into coverage. I had all day to throw. Adam beat his man and made a great catch. We were off and running.

Playing in that game reminded me a bit of when I was at the University of Houston—up-tempo, aggressive, and in sync. Everybody was making plays and we were feeding off each other's energy. I completed 25 of 33 passes, set my career high with 369 yards, and tossed three touchdowns. We won, 34–17.

Afterward Coach Mike Zimmer gathered the team. "I don't usually do this," said Zimmer as he clutched a football in the air. "But, game ball, Case Keenum!" I only saw him give out a game ball in the locker room one other time all season. The team erupted and mobbed me.

I loved it. Nothing compares to that feeling. Jumping up and down with the guys after pouring out everything on the field. It was a huge pile . . . even owner Zygi Wilf got into the action. After we settled down a little, I got a chance to speak to the team. "I love you boys," I said. "I haven't been around many teams like this. I'm so proud of you guys. I'm going to fight for you boys every day."

From that point on, we were a cohesive unit, and we were going to be tough to beat.

It started with the line. They played so well against Tampa Bay and kept it going all year long. I can't say enough nice things about this group. We actually went five games in a row without giving up a sack. Props to O-line coach Tony Sparano (the former Miami Dolphins head coach) and those big boys up front. Big guys never get enough credit, but those guys were *good*.

The receiving corps was just like me—flying under the radar but ready to show the world what they could do. Thielen, Diggs, Wright, tight end Kyle Rudolph, running backs Jerick McKinnon and Latavius Murray—we all took different paths to get here, and now that we were here together, we were going to take advantage.

Thielen was so much like me, people would confuse the two of us in public all the time. Like me, Adam, who went to nearby Minnesota State, was an undrafted free agent. People would ask me questions as if I were Adam. I got tired of explaining that I wasn't and just started answering as Adam. "I'm doing great. I would be even better if that Case Keenum guy would throw me the ball more." Adam did the same thing . . . so if a medium-height white guy claiming to be me said something weird to you at a Timberwolves game last year, it was probably him.

Teams spend millions of dollars scouting players, but they can't account for chemistry. The 2017 Vikings had it. Our defense was loaded with young talent. I knew pretty quickly that we were going to have a special season. As we started racking up wins—Chicago, Baltimore, Green Bay, Cleveland—we were all feeling good about how the team fit with me at quarterback. Everyone, except maybe one person . . . Zimmer.

Even when we were in the midst of an eight-game win streak, Zimmer didn't seem sure who he wanted to start at quarterback. In Week 10, I threw for 304 yards and four touchdowns in a 38–30 win over the Redskins. I threw two interceptions as well— definitely bad decisions—but felt good about how the offense played. Then, on Monday, Zimmer wouldn't say that I was the starter. Privately, I wasn't told anything one way or the other. Zimmer was letting the public think that he was mulling over playing Teddy. That particular week, my former team, the Rams, were coming to Minnesota on Sunday. Of course I wanted to play. But I had learned there were things I couldn't control. I just kept my head down and worked as if I would be the starter.

One early morning I was in the facility studying when Coach Zimmer called me upstairs. "Why did your agents call [general manager] Rick Spielman to ask what was going on?" he asked. Coach wanted to know if I was angry that he hadn't named me the starter yet.

"I honestly don't know, Coach," I said. I had empowered my agents to do their job. They don't check with me every time before making calls. To be honest, asking why he wouldn't name me the starter in public was a valid question. My agents were doing their job. They were curious what his motives were. We were winning. I was playing really well. Maybe he was trying to motivate me, or the team. If so, he wasn't telling me that was the reason.

I told Zimmer that I was going to do my job regardless of what the status of the QB competition was. Coach Zimmer respected that, and we ended that meeting on a positive note. I'm not sure if he even officially announced me as the starter all the way up until the NFC championship game. Don't get me wrong. I know my role as a player. I know what is and isn't my job. I always try to do what I'm coached to do and to be the best player and teammate I can be.

I also have no idea the pressures a head coach faces. I loved playing for Zimmer and like many of the great coaches I've had, I would still try to run through a brick wall for him if he asked. But I will say that as a quarterback there is plenty going on in our heads already. We have a lot on our plate each week. This little distraction became almost a joke each week in the media. I had to answer the same questions again and again—one more thing buzzing around that I had to block out. I have to admit I would have appreciated less buzzing. A little job security goes a long way.

During this time, I started to forge a wonderful relationship with the Vikings' long-time team chaplain Tom Lamphere. I met with Tom weekly, and he had a real knack for giving not just spiritual guidance, but real practical advice for the kinds of challenges football players face. Tom would always ask how much sleep I was getting because he knew how important sleep is to athletic performance. He also focused on trying to make us better people, which, as it always turns out, makes guys better football players.

With all this noise buzzing around me, Tom advised me on how to stay centered. He told me to hold on to two truths in my life:

1. God has you right where He wants you. He has put you exactly where He intended to. And He has equipped you for that time.

2. It is your job to do as much as you can with the talents God has given you. To prepare as well as you can for the challenges ahead. Once you do that, you can rest easy at night.

> For God has not given us a spirit of fear, but one of power, love, and sound judgment.
> —2 Timothy 1:7

If I hold on to these two truths, I have nothing to worry about. I knew in my heart that I had prepared the very best I knew how. I had given everything I had every day. I rested easy at night and had confidence to step in between those white lines every Sunday.

———

Eventually Zimmer did give me the nod for at least the game against the Rams. My former team was playing really well with Jared Goff under center and it was a big game. I'm not going to lie, I wanted to beat them. I wanted to win *really bad.* Zimmer actually pulled me aside to make sure I didn't get too jacked up. I was pumped and he knew it.

That week Coach Stefanski came up with a great plan for me to keep things simple and stick to the process.

Keep doing what I do. Don't press.

As you get older you realize more and more, your dad was right: *Pray hard, play hard, take care of the football, have fun.*

It was great advice. I actually prepared mentally early in the week for what it would be like to play against many of my former teammates, who were my friends and knew me well. I was able to totally ignore defensive lineman Michael Brockers and Aaron Donald when they yelled, "Don't act like you don't know us! Come on, Case! Let us come say hi." I just walked back to the huddle and didn't say a word. They didn't get the chance to get reacquainted because they didn't record a single sack all game. Beating the Rams 24–7 was incredibly sweet. And by sweet, I mean it felt *really* good. But, no time to gloat. We had a short week, because we were facing the Lions on Thanksgiving Day in Detroit.

Like many Americans, football has been a huge part of Thanksgiving my entire life, only usually I was *watching* it on TV with my family and then re-creating the game's big plays in the backyard, not *playing* on TV.

Growing up in Texas, I was a Cowboys fan, and naturally, a big Troy Aikman fan. The holiday was even more fun when they won and Aikman had a big game. I love and cherish those times with my family and Kimberly's family through the years. So playing at Ford Field that Thursday was pretty special. By this point of the season, everyone on the offense had started to become really comfortable with each other. I knew I could trust the line. And I knew my receivers were going to make plays if I gave them a chance. We were scoring a lot and having fun celebrating with each other. In the first quarter I ran in a 9-yard touchdown and we all sat in a circle in the end zone and pretended to be eating a Thanksgiving dinner. I politely mimed scooping out some mashed potatoes and passed the imaginary bowl to my left to Kyle Rudolph. Thank God the NFL had loosened up its rules on celebrating, because that one was pretty elaborate (and fun). Then again, who doesn't like a Thanksgiving meal? I couldn't be in Abilene, but this wasn't a bad place to be on the holiday.

We went on to beat the Lions 30–24, and after the game, Fox asked me to do an interview with Troy Aikman. My friend Zac, a diehard Cowboys fan, texted me afterward "Did you ever think you'd be saying 'Thanks, Troy' after beating the Lions on Thanksgiving?" I don't know if I had ever had that specific thought. I did know I was going to enjoy it. That was the kind of season we were having.

By the end of the regular season, even if Zimmer didn't make a formal declaration, there was no debate about who the starter was going to be. Now the media was left to ponder who would be the backup, Bradford or Bridgewater. We finished the season at 13–3, NFC North champions. I was headed to the playoffs. I was excited as all get-out. I didn't know what was coming next, but I knew it was going to be different. I had never started a playoff game in the NFL. I had an idea God might have something special in store for me.

Turns out, He had a miracle in mind.

Chapter 15

SKOL

I described what happened in the divisional playoffs in the prologue. What a way to kick off my postseason career. But the madness didn't stop after Diggs crossed the goal line.

In the midst of the mayhem after the Minneapolis Miracle, I feel someone tap me on the shoulder. It's referee Tony Corrente and he wants to inform me that we have to run another play. *We have to do what?* I'm still running around grabbing guys and yelling who knows what. *How are we going to run another play?* There are literally hundreds of people on the field. I have no idea where any of my offensive teammates are.

Then I see Pat Shurmur and tell him we have to run another play. He told me to just find ten guys and take a knee (*phew . . .* looks like Kimberly gets her kneel-down). Now instead of looking for guys to hug I'm looking for guys wearing helmets who can line up. I tell Kai Forbath and punter Ryan Quigley that they may have to come back in. They wanted no part of that.

Somehow we get it together enough to line up for one more play. The Saints have all gone into the locker room and we are waiting for eleven guys to come out to line up. I'm still milling around as the officials are trying to sort everything out when I see my face on the big screen in U.S. Bank Stadium. Without even thinking, I raise my hands above my head and clap, mimicking the SKOL chant I've seen all season long in Minnesota. It's the crowd's Nordic war cry, and it never fails to get everyone fired up. If you've ever been to a game at Vikings stadium, you know what I'm talking about. It gives me goose bumps just thinking about it. I wanted to see if I could get one started. The first clap . . . nothing happens. Then on the second . . . *BOOM* . . . the whole building erupts, "SKOL . . . SKOL . . . SKOL."

It got so loud, Kyle Rudolph came over and said we were going to have to go silent with our snap count, something you usually don't have to do when the quarterback is under center. Especially in your home stadium. By the time we actually ran the play, over eight minutes had passed since Diggs's touchdown. The NFL actually changed the rules in the offseason to make sure this situation never happens again. Now, when a team wins a game with a touchdown as time expires, they don't have to try an extra point.

After the celebration finally started to settle down, I ran toward the locker room. I was on such a high, I honestly don't even remember exactly what Coach Zimmer said to us. I'm sure it was awesome. The locker room atmosphere is so much fun after a win. This particular locker room was the best I've ever been in. As soon as Coach was done, guys were hugging, crying, a lot of "can you believe what just happened?" I remember sitting down in my locker after I had made my rounds with the team and thinking, *I want to see Kimberly right now.* I went straight out of the locker room before I even took my pads off because I wanted to see my family so badly. I gave huge hugs to Kimberly, Mom, Dad, and my sisters Lauren and Allison. I wanted to share the whole experience with them, so I took my family with me to the media room where the podium is for postgame interviews. I love having them with me in those moments.

After that, I had one last interview at my locker with longtime NFL reporter Peter King. We were trying to talk, but every other second my iPhone let out a "Ding." Peter is asking me to describe the play and I can barely think because my phone is making such a racket. After good games, I'll get a fair number of texts. Maybe a few dozen. After a bad game, I might get just two—Mom and Dr. Young. On this night, it was *546 texts.*

After Peter got what he needed, I got dressed and dashed out of the stadium as soon as I could. We had big plans to celebrate with our friends and families at a downtown Minneapolis restaurant. By now, it was dumping snow. Thank God the Vikings play indoors. We left our car next to the stadium and got right out. Everyone else struggled to escape the parking lot. Turns out, we beat our whole party to the restaurant by a good bit. That's when things got off the rails for just a little while.

Kimberly and I discussed what to do after the game earlier in the week. You can't exactly make a reservation for fifty-five people. She said she would take care of it and even visited the restaurant earlier in the week to make sure it could accommodate our whole party. The manager there during the week said no problem. They were going to put us down in the basement, where we could have privacy and enjoy ourselves. But when we arrived, it was nothing like what the restaurant had promised. The basement was filled wall to wall with people and they were playing loud, thumping club music. My party was more of a soft jazz crowd.

The host shuffled us down into the basement in the spot we were supposed to go. Only, we never imagined all these people. Everyone started to realize who I was and the chaos intensified. Cell phones came flying out and people were chanting "SKOL . . . SKOL . . . SKOL." That was awesome in the stadium, but right now it wasn't what I had in mind. Kimberly was not happy. She had even pre-ordered appetizers so our friends and family could come right in and have a nice time. Now there's no way they could even make their way through the throngs of people.

"Case," Kimberly said, "We gotta go. Everyone is staring at us."

"Where are my boys at?" I asked. I wanted to celebrate . . . with people I knew.

"I don't know," she said. "This isn't what the restaurant said was going to happen at all."

Finally, we tracked down a manager and explained the situation. Luckily, he had a Plan B. Instead of the basement, he moved us up to the first floor just as most of the party, including my guys, finally showed up. The restaurant was very accommodating, actually setting up some people to run interference around our area. Trust me, I've never needed guards in a public setting. Fighting off the paparazzi is not something you really think much about growing up in Abilene. Usually I can slip right in and out of any place no problem. But tonight was an exception in every way possible.

When I look back on that day, I remember not wanting to leave the field, because I wanted that moment to last. I wanted the night to last forever. But it didn't. Nothing that happens on the football field does. Only one thing does . . . only one thing is eternal. That's your relationship with the

Lord. That's why I answered the sideline reporter's question the way I did.

The week after the Minneapolis Miracle is a blur. We went to Philadelphia and lost the NFC title game to the Eagles 38–7. It was one of those games where things just didn't come together. I certainly didn't perform anywhere near my best. Plays that had worked all season were just a little bit off. We started the game with a 9-play, 75-yard touchdown drive. I hit Kyle Rudolph in the end zone and we actually had a 7–0 lead. But on the next drive, Eagles defensive end Chris Long hit my throwing arm on a pass intended for Thielen that resulted in a 50-yard pick-six. I don't believe the two teams were that lopsided. Sometimes momentum just starts rolling one way and never turns back.

Everyone on the team was acutely aware of what was happening in Minneapolis in two weeks. We desperately wanted to reward the fan base with the league's first-ever home Super Bowl game. Wasn't meant to be. We were disappointed, of course. But so much good has come out of that season, not just the Minneapolis Miracle. It allowed me and my teammates to talk about our faith and what's really important to us. And just like most fans, it's a day I'll never forget. I am going to be eternally grateful to Minnesota. If it wasn't for the chance the team gave me, I would never have gotten the opportunity to take the next step in my life.

Chapter 16

Bronco Country

For some reason, my agents decided to start the call off with the bad news. March 12 was the first day of free agency. We could finally end weeks of speculation and watching way too many sports talk shows on ESPN and reading way too many articles from "experts." It was time to talk about real offers.

Kimberly and I were staying in a small town outside Houston and this particular afternoon, driving downtown with our friends Ginny and Carter to attend the Rockets game. I was the team's guest of honor and got to shoot a ceremonial free throw for charity before tip-off. I'm sitting in typical traffic on Highway 59 and it's time to find out what's next.

Jeff Nalley and Graylan Crain with the Select Sports Group, who had represented me since I left college, called and began by telling me the Vikings hadn't come around yet.

I knew there was a strong possibility I wasn't returning to Minnesota. The team had a window to negotiate with me before free agency started since I was under contract from the previous season. They didn't make an offer or place the franchise tag on me. I had read the reports they were interested in Redskins quarterback Kirk Cousins, but you never know how these things will actually play out. I had talked to Kirk, who is a great guy, and I knew other teams were interested in him as well.

I had a strong sense that multiple teams would be involved. We did our homework on several teams. Staying in Minnesota made sense because of familiarity with the offense and the city. I knew it might not happen, but to actually hear it was a little tougher than I expected. I leaned my head back on the car seat and thought, *Oh boy, here we go again.*

A year before, after the 2016 season, I didn't think I was going to get signed for a starting job. But I had some success with the Rams and won some games. I figured I'd have solid options to sign with a team as a backup. The first night of free agency, I checked in with my agents. They told me to sit tight, nothing yet, but it shouldn't be long. OK, it's only one night. Nothing to worry about. The next day, no word. *Is my phone working?*

Part of me wanted to check in every five minutes with my agents. I knew that wouldn't help and tried to go about my business, working out, playing a little golf, spending time with Kimberly. I'm sure I wasn't fooling anyone. My agents tried to keep me upbeat, saying teams were interested, I'd just have to wait a little bit to see how the market shook out.

One day turned into two and before I knew it, we were a week into free agency. No offer. Finally, two weeks after the 2017 free agency period started, my agents called and said the Vikings were ready to make an offer. It was difficult waiting, but once again, God had a plan for me. Several doors closed, but one opened for me that would propel my career to the next level. Every time it's the right one.

———

Back to 2018. This offseason was different. I knew I would get offers. But the same fears were there. We're all afraid of the unknown. Maybe it's uncertainty about whether an NFL team wants me, or whether my job is safe, or whether I'm going to pass this test in school next week. We want to know everything is going to work out. It's difficult to trust when you can't see.

I'm not sure how truly present I was in that moment . . . part of me was worried about the traffic and getting to the game on the time. Another part was concerned that the right kind of offer wouldn't come. Joining a competitive team was important. I had experienced a lot of winning in Minnesota and wanted to keep it going.

In the days leading up to free agency I had been linked to almost every team that needed a quarterback. I didn't know if any of that was going to happen. But I had been here before. Facing uncertainty and not sure who wanted me and who believed in me. All I knew for sure was that God had taken care of me every time before. And I was sure He would put me in the right place once again.

I'm not sure everyone realizes how beneficial good agents can be. There's a reason they're the ones talking to teams. Through the years, I'm sure there were plenty of league executives who had things to say about me that weren't very nice. They're in the business of keeping players' salaries down so they can fit in as much talent as possible under the salary cap. And some of them probably just didn't like me as a player. Unless you're Aaron Rodgers or Tom Brady, that's how it goes. The agents act as a shield for the players. Jeff and Graylan know me so well, I completely trust them to speak for me. And I know they're going to bring me back information that is helpful to me, not just the white noise that is everywhere that time of year.

On this night they thought I would want to know about the Vikings first. Makes sense, even if it didn't make me feel better. What happened next is one of those moments you'd like to look back at and say was more dramatic, but in reality it happened faster than I expected. They said matter-of-factly that the Denver Broncos wanted to make a two- or possibly three-year offer.

OK guys, why didn't you lead with that?

Like everyone else my age, I was a huge John Elway fan. I had his jersey when I was a kid and thought he was the coolest. When he scrambled and got spun around like a helicopter in Super Bowl XXXII, he still led the team to the win. He was the man.

I first had the honor of meeting him at the 2009 Walter Camp Awards ceremony. My parents couldn't come to that event so I had my buddy Mikado tag along as my plus-one. He recently reminded me exactly how the conversation went down when I walked up to Elway to introduce myself.

"Mr. Elway, my name is Case Keenum," I mumbled. "It's a real honor to meet you."

"Oh, man. I love watching you sling the ball around at Houston," Elway said.

"I didn't even know you knew who I was," I replied, for no helpful reason.

Now, Elway is the general manager and VP of Football Operations for the Broncos and he wants *me*? I couldn't believe it. But my agents weren't done. They went straight back to business mode and started running down all the other situations around the league. And then they said, "By the way, the Broncos basically need to know right now."

Denver wasn't in on Kirk and didn't want to wait around for him. My agents said we shouldn't wait either. We have a team that wants you and wants you bad. "I think this is going to be the best option for more than just financial reasons," Jeff said.

I had so many questions. I was spinning every possible scenario in rapid fire. Kimberly, who tends to be more expressive about these kinds of issues—and every other kind of issue, too—cut us off. "Wait, the Denver Broncos . . . we're excited about this, right? Why aren't we screaming right now?"

OK, OK . . . we're getting somewhere.

A little less business and a little more whooping was appropriate. At this point, we pulled off the highway and I moved over to the passenger seat so I could keep talking. After reviewing each situation some more, my agents decide to give me some time to think about the options.

"How about fifteen minutes?"

Fifteen minutes? I'm supposed to make a decision that will shape my career and affect both me and my family for years. Jeff and Graylan said they were going to circle back with other teams that were interested to try to get the complete picture. They would hit me back shortly. The sooner I could decide on Denver, the better.

We sat in traffic and prayed for the strength to follow God's will and make the right choice. I knew almost instantly that I wanted to be a Bronco. But there's so much to consider—the team around you, coaches, situation, organization...I wanted to be really certain, because I hoped my next team would be my last in the NFL. I wanted to play for one team for a long time. Jeff said something interesting early on when I was preparing for free agency and we thought we would field multiple offers. "You'll know in your gut which is the right one." I needed a little good counsel and there was none better than my father. I called Dad from the car.

No answer.

Didn't he know I had to make this decision? Wasn't he on Twitter? Didn't he read Profootballtalk.com? I tried him again. Still no answer. Where was he? What could possibly be more important than this?

I found out later he was on the treadmill and didn't have his phone on him. Apparently, the rest of the world kept on moving even though I had to make one of the most important decisions of my life!

By now, I had arrived at the Toyota Center and had to go out in front of eighteen thousand people to shoot this free throw. Make no mistake—I know I have game. I was an all-state basketball player in high school. I stepped to the line, took one dribble, and took my shot . . . nothing but net. Maybe Houston coach Mike D'Antoni was watching, and I could add a 10-day contract with the Rockets into the mix. Later that night, on Fox 26, sports anchor Mark Berman said when they showed the highlight, "Is there anything Case Keenum can't do?" I appreciate that, but to be honest, I was pretty stressed out at the time. My brief display of basketball skill did little to distract me. I'm smiling and waving to the crowd and wondering whether I'm going to agree to a contract with a new team tonight.

Throughout the game, I'm texting people in my inner circle, thinking, overthinking. I should be watching the game because James Harden and the Rockets are a lot of fun. Instead, I'm staring at my phone waiting for new information. The more I think about Denver, the more excited I become. In the weeks since the season, I had done a lot of due diligence on the teams that might be looking at adding a quarterback. I talked to players and former coaches. All the feedback I heard on Denver was incredibly positive.

It was a first-rate organization from top to bottom. Head coach Vance Joseph had been a defensive backs coach for the Texans when I played there. We had kept up through the years, and I knew he would be a guy I would love to play for. They had great talent on offense like receivers Demaryius Thomas and Emmanuel Sanders. Their new offensive coordinator Bill Musgrave was supposed to be a brilliant game-planner who would fit well with my game. And John Elway ran the team. John Elway!

We leave the game and head home. At this point, Kimberly and I are all about Denver. It's about 10 o'clock and I'm checking my phone and seeing if any apparel stores are still open. I'm ready to go to the mall and start buying orange shirts. (I'm not a big "go to the mall guy," so that should show you how excited I was.) But Jeff and Graylan haven't called us back. I'm trying to stay cool. Kimberly . . . not so much.

"We blew it. They're not calling us back. I don't know where we're going to land now. We should have just said yes on the spot."

I tried to tell her that's not how it works. Jeff and Graylan would make sure the team didn't move on before hearing our answer. At least I thought that's how it works. I said that to comfort Kimberly, and maybe myself a little bit.

It reached 11 p.m. and *still*, no word back. I wasn't sure that sitting and staring at the phone would do any good, so I decided that I might as well go to bed. I was working out in the morning. Kimberly and I are sitting in bed having already brushed our teeth, ready to turn off the lights, when Jeff and Graylan finally call.

"We talked to everybody. The Broncos really want you. We think it's a great fit. What do you think?"

"Let's do this!" Kimberly and I both said.

Jeff and Graylan said, "OK, we'll make it happen." They also made one thing very clear . . . I couldn't tell anyone. Not even my family. The Broncos wanted to break the news. That was tough for Kimberly and me. We're close to our families and wanted to share the great news. Kimberly and I decided we had to celebrate. But how? It was 1:30 a.m. and we were out in the middle of nowhere in this house we rented for the offseason. For some reason, this house had robes in the bathroom. I'm not a robe guy (OK, maybe I am a robe guy, but I'm not a *mall* guy). They just seemed so fitting for this moment. So we put on our robes, heated up the left-over pizza we had for dinner the night before, and toasted with cans of LaCroix seltzer water. Not exactly crystal and stretch limousines, but it fit Kimberly and me.

Before I even woke up, my phone was blowing up. Adam Schefter had Tweeted out the news. "The Broncos will sign free-agent quarterback Case Keenum." My dad was nowhere to be found when I needed his help last night, but apparently he was all ears for Adam Schefter!

I'm so thrilled with how free agency worked out. When I arrived in Denver a few days later for my introductory press conference, I knew in my gut I had made the right decision. The moment we stepped off the plane and saw the Rocky Mountains on the horizon, it felt like the right place. Everyone was incredibly welcoming. From the Broncos staff, to the coaches, to the front office. At one point during the crazy day of signing the contract, meeting staff, media requests, press conferences, and house-hunting, Kimberly was talking to an assistant who works upstairs. She told Kimberly that she had been praying for us to come to Denver all along.

One door shut in Minnesota. But God left another one open for me to walk through. I had a few stressful hours in the process, but all along I knew I was in good hands. It's taken me a while to figure it out. But all the best things in my life have not come easy. Looking back, all those tough times make the good times—like these—that much better.

Chapter 17

Why I Play

The Minneapolis Miracle? Where does it rank among the moments of my life? My answer to the sideline reporter when he thrust the microphone in my face and asked if it was the best:

> "It's probably going to go down as the third-best moment of my life, behind giving my life to Jesus Christ and marrying my wife."

If you saw me smiling from ear to ear on TV that evening, you may not believe that statement.

You might say: *Case, didn't you write that you had dreamed of this moment since you were a kid?* If my postgame statement seems hypocritical, I promise, that's because you still don't know me well enough yet. And you definitely don't know my wife, Kimberly. If you'd been there on our wedding day and seen her walk down the aisle, or if you'd spent every day with her since, *then* you'd understand why my marriage ranks higher than that play. Trust me, it's no contest.

As for giving my life to Christ, I don't see how anything can be placed above that. If you have a strong relationship with Jesus Christ, then you understand why that's *always* No. 1. If you know that you are loved by Jesus unconditionally, if you are abiding in Him daily, if you have an unexplainable peace inside and know that He's there for you in good times and in bad, then you understand. If you have a relationship with Christ that's filled with complete and eternal joy, how can anything else compete?

I am a Christian athlete, not an athlete who happens to be Christian. Sometimes being a Christian athlete gets a bad rap.

Oh, he's a Christian; he's soft.

I don't think that's the case at all. Christ makes up for our weaknesses and makes us stronger. Throughout my career, there have been a lot of people who didn't think I was good enough. And they were almost right.

By myself, I'm not good enough. On my own, I'm not a good enough husband. On my own, I'm not a good enough football player. On my own, I fail. But when we stop trying to do life on our own, when we ask Jesus to be the Lord and Savior of our life, it all changes. With Christ's help, we *become* good enough. Not because of something we have done, but because of what He has done. We are no longer sitting on the throne of our own life. We put Christ there. We've changed positions. We stop making decisions based solely on what we want, and we start living to glorify Christ in everything we do. When we do this, God does something unbelievable. When we change from trusting in ourselves to trusting in Him, He sends His Holy Spirit to live inside of us. *Crazy!*

The Spirit of the living God is inside His believers! I think God likes to flex His muscles and show off in our weaknesses. He looks down on me and says, "I got this, dude. He claims Me, I'm going to claim him right back."

> I have been crucified with Christ and I no longer live, but Christ lives in me. The life I now live in the body, I live by faith in the Son of God, who loved me and gave himself for me. —Galatians 2:20

I've described plenty of big plays on the field. And those were all so fun and special. But in the end, when it really comes down to it, they only matter for *one reason.*

Because those performances gave me the chance to glorify God.

He put me in this position. He gave me these abilities and pointed me in the direction to apply them. I just worked as hard as I could and prayed to follow His will.

One of my favorite movies is *Chariots of Fire*, the 1981 Oscar-winning film about track athletes competing in the 1924 Olympics. One of the runners, Eric Liddell, struggled to reconcile competing with his Christian beliefs. He tried to explain to his sister why he ran: "I believe God made me for a purpose. But He also made me fast. And when I run I feel His pleasure."

That's exactly how I feel. I play to honor and please Him. Any success I have is because of Him. That's why I was so happy to pronounce my faith on national television after the Minneapolis Miracle. It was true then just as much that day as it was the day I tore my ACL. It may not have been the only thing on my mind as I lay on the turf at the Rose Bowl, or the only thought I had when I ran around like a crazy person at U.S. Bank Stadium. But it was in my heart and it came out during the interview. As one of my good friends Jon Randles, a pastor from West Texas, used to say, "You *is* what you *is*, and you *ooze* what you *ooze*. When you're squeezed, what's inside of you is going to come out." When pressure is applied, when it comes down to crunch time, the real you is going to come out. What's the real you?

That's why I wrote this book. I hope others will see that the reason I've been able to do some things on the football field is because I gave my life to Christ. In turn, Christ lives in me. It's a simple formula that has guided me my whole life. I don't want you to think that this is my secret formula for success as a football player. Being a Christian isn't easy. And life as a Christian is not always going to lead to a life of winning and worldly success.

Please don't think I'm saying if you have Christ in your corner, you will make it wherever you are trying to go. I'm saying if you give your life to Christ, your definition for success will change. Christ's view is quite different than the world's in a lot of respects . . .

> "How narrow is the gate and difficult the road
> that leads to life, and few find it." —Matthew 7:14

> "Note this: Some who are last will be first, and
> some who are first will be last." —Luke 13:30

In my opinion, living a life *with* and *for* Christ is far better than anything else I could imagine. That's why the best moment of my life might not be what you think. It wasn't the miracle pass that beat the Saints on January 14, 2018. It's not any of the passes I'm going to throw the rest of my career. The most miraculous thing in my life is the gospel living itself out in me every day.

I realize everyone may not get a chance to throw game-winning touchdown passes in the NFL playoffs or run onto the field with fireworks and fighter jets overhead. But there is something more out there. Something greater. If there is one thing in this book I want you to understand, if there's one thing I want you to take away, it's this: *God's love is available to anyone.*

You might be saying to yourself, "Well, if you only knew the real me, how messed up I am, and . . ." You don't have to clean up your life first! God wants to meet you right where you are. It doesn't matter how far you feel you are from God right now. He wants you. Just the way you are. Just like His power is infinite, so are His love and mercy.

I'm sure thankful His mercy and grace are boundless because I keep seeming to find new ways to screw up. But God doesn't have failure in mind for us. God wants everyone to succeed. I think that I would be just as happy in any other profession with Christ in my life. If that was the plan for me, then I am confident I would find joy in it.

Maybe that's why the Lord has carved out this specific windy path for me. Maybe I wouldn't have learned what He wanted to teach me any other way! Sure, it may have been extremely hard when I was in some of those low moments.

I may not have been able to see the good in any of what was going on around me. I may have been close to throwing in the towel and giving up. But looking back, I can see God's fingerprints in every area of my life. I want people to know that. If I was 6′ 4″ and got scholarship offers from every college in the nation and then went on to be the top pick in the draft, would my story reach people in the same way? I don't know. I'll admit, there were times I wished all that was the case. But now I'm glad I had to take a harder route to the NFL. I'm thankful for the tough times in my life. I honestly can say that. When I first hurt my knee in college, I was devastated. Devastation turned to hopelessness, but God comforted me through His Word and friends and family, and that despair turned around to hope. Then to resolve. Then to thankfulness. And finally, joy.

It's been an incredible journey. And this journey through the University of Houston, the Texans, the Rams, the Texans again, the Rams again . . . oh, you know the story by now . . . has taught me so much about humility and trusting that God has a plan for all of us. And it's perfect.

> "For I know the plans I have for you," declares the LORD, "plans to prosper you and not to harm you, plans to give you hope and a future." —Jeremiah 29:11 (NIV)

I've always thought it's easy to point up to the heavens and give glory to God after winning the game or throwing a touchdown. It's a different story when things aren't going well. All these times are what has made me into the person I am today. And I know that God made me to do exactly what I'm doing right now. It's my job to do the best I can and keep pointing up at Him. Good times and bad.

I have no idea what will happen in Denver. I sure would like to win a lot of football games. I want to reward the Broncos' faith in me and be a part of the incredible community in this city. I want to experience that feeling you get when you're jumping up and down with the guys in the locker room. Of almost having to cover your ears because 80,000 people are yelling, screaming, and cheering their heads off. Or hugging Kimberly and my family after the game and sharing my joy with them. Sounds like a game plan to me. But I'm also aware that God sometimes has a different agenda. I might not always be comfortable with it. It might not be as easy as I'd sometimes like it to be. The funny thing is, it's almost always better than I imagined. I am so fired up to see what's next.

So, for all of you out there who have been told you can't. For those who think you aren't good enough to live a life fully surrendered to Christ. If you've been overlooked your whole life, if you've worked hard and not seen anything come of it.

I've been there. This book has been my journey. Your journey, similar to mine, yet so different I'm sure, means just as much. We are in the journey of life together, we are here to bring glory to God and love those around us. Playing football is my passion, but it's not who I am. I'm playing for my King.

I'm playing for more.

Afterword

featuring Kimberly Keenum

One of the best parts of the Minneapolis Miracle is people coming up to me and telling me *exactly* where they were when it happened. It doesn't matter where I am. It could be the airport, the post office, in line at Starbucks— someone will share what they were doing at that moment.

I *love* hearing those stories. It reminds me how many people are touched by what we do on the field. There's a video out there of different fan reactions that is unbelievable. A guy runs right out of his house and jumps into the pool while fully clothed. Others are crying. Everyone is screaming. Most of it is nonsensical, just like I was that day. One of my favorites is Michael Strahan jumping out of his chair in a suit that probably costs more than my truck on the FOX Postgame set. His cohosts look at him like he's lost his mind as he jumps around pumping his fists.

It's easy to forget how much a sporting event can move people. I want to share one particular fan's reaction.

Granted, this fan had a little more at stake than most. But afterward there was no one I wanted to talk to more than Kimberly. I wanted to hear every detail from her perspective. Luckily, she keeps an in-depth journal of our life in the NFL. This is her story of the Minneapolis Miracle:

———

It took me hours to arrange, but I had everyone placed just right in the "family section" of U.S. Bank Stadium. We had sixty people in town for the playoff game—way more than we had ever hosted for an NFL game. I had my brothers, Brandon and Brian, strategically placed in front, my childhood best friend Bethany to my left, my parents, Keith and Diana, and Case's parents to my right. Then a whole other group of friends right behind me. I had my crew there to protect me so I could focus on my guy.

I had the same seat each game and always knew where my close friends on the team were sitting. Knowing that they were there and that they understood the highs and lows of the game added an extra bit of comfort for me. It was a special bond with each of them that grew throughout the season. I made sure to be sitting close to Kelly Remmers, whose husband was an offensive lineman and always protected Case—obviously important. Caitlin Thielen and I had our air high-fives down when Case and Adam connected on a pass. Tight end David Morgan's girlfriend, Langlie, and long snapper Kevin McDermott's wife, Lauren, were always close by and a huge support all season.

Case had been talking about how he wanted the ball in his hands in the final minutes of a game. He's so competitive and that desire was fueling him all week long. He dreamed of that moment. He believed he could do it. I would always joke that I preferred kneeling in victory formation at the end of games rather than passing, because that meant we had the game in hand already. A lot of games that season had ended with Case kneeling or already out of the game because they had the game locked up in the last few minutes. In those moments, I am able to relax and enjoy watching. But Case was craving a moment like this.

We were down 21–20 with three minutes left. This was Case's moment. The big drive.

My heart was beating out of my chest. I wanted it for him so badly. All the friends and family around me wanted it as well. So did the entire stadium. You could almost feel the air leave the entire Vikings crowd as every person was holding their breath for him.

Case drives down the field and we get in position to kick a field goal with 1:29 left on the clock—a 53-yarder.

Wow, I don't think I realized how far a 53-yard field goal was until I saw where they were lined up right in front of me!

Kai Forbath made it.

Case finally did it. He had his drive to win the game. It was huge. We were up 24–23 with 1:29 left to go. We have the best defense in the league. All we need is one more stop.

The Saints only had a minute to do something, but Drew Brees is one heck of a QB.

The Saints drove right down the field. It was brutal to watch. I started to think, *What if we lose?* I tried to make note of what was going on around me. I thought this could be Case's last time playing as a Viking, wearing No. 7 in purple with everyone cheering for him in this gorgeous stadium. We are free agents after this season and very well could have an opportunity to play somewhere else.

Everyone is on their feet.

All the purple.

The beautiful windows at the end zone. They were dark and gloomy that day with snow just coming down.

I saw all the rally flags high in the air cheering on the defense. Somehow, Drew blocked it all out and drove his team down for the game-winning field goal.

When New Orleans scored, I was afraid that was it, time was not in our favor. I thought that Case had done his job. Don't get me wrong; I wanted this win so badly. But I was trying to justify a loss in my mind just so I could get through it. I was proud of him.

But we did have 25 seconds . . . 25 seconds. Was that enough time to go win this game? Could we do it again?

Oh man, I wish we could go kneel and win. I still can see the wave of purple and everyone on their feet. The stadium was silent. Everyone had hope, but we all knew time was against us. Vikings history is full of playoff let-downs, and this fan base has definitely endured more than their fair share of heartbreak. *Please, Lord, not again,* I prayed with thousands of Vikings faithful.

I asked my brothers how many plays could we get off? I had an idea, but I needed the affirmation. *"We can do this, Kimberly,"* Brandon said. "He has time. He can probably get three or four plays off."

When I am nervous, I am usually really quiet. I most likely won't talk to anyone or even make eye contact. My eyes are just on Case wherever he is.

The most comforting people to talk to in this type of situation are other players' wives. They get it. I'm constantly clasping my hands around my mouth and saying, *"You got this, Case." "You can do this." "Take care of the ball." "Be smart." "See the field."* If the team is in a high-stress situation, I'm saying these things over and over again. I have to remember to breathe.

I'm so ready for the next play, to see something good happen. When good things happen, I start to calm down and just enjoy watching. Case always tries to tell me to enjoy myself. I've worked on that a lot. To just trust him, trust the process. To know he worked his tail off and no matter the outcome, I will be so proud of him.

Twenty seconds left. I am praying for the Lord to do something big. *Let Case shine bright for You, Lord.*

I'm praying for safety, I am praying the receivers to catch the ball, for the line to protect him. I'm praying for a win. I am. I know probably the Lord doesn't really care about that part of it all, but I'm praying for it anyway this Sunday.

I am locked on No. 7. We call a time-out and we have 18 seconds left to go. Case throws it to Jarius Wright, who gets tripped up and falls down. Incomplete pass. No gain on the play. No more time outs. Now we are at 14 seconds to go.

It is second-and-10 at our 39. Another incompletion. We only had 10 seconds left. I can honestly say that I thought it was over. I hate to admit it. I never give up and I always believe. Always. But I thought this was the end. I wish I didn't think that in that moment but we were at the 39-yard line, too far back to make a field goal.

If we had to leave the stadium that day without the win, I would be OK. But somewhere in my brain, I thought, *Case can do this.* I thought, *Just one more good throw, Case. Just one and let's get that field goal.*

Check in with my brothers—can we get in position for a field goal? They say yes. It might be the longest field goal ever, but it was something to hope for. The ball is snapped, Case throws it deep to Diggs, and the most epic play in NFL playoff game history happens.

Diggs does the miraculous. He jumps and he catches it. He lands in-bounds. Everyone in the stands is yelling at him to get out-of-bounds! But I don't hear them. The thought quickly comes into my mind: *Why is he still in-bounds?*

Oh. My. Gosh. The guy missed him.

I'm getting excited, but I'm not really getting it. I think I must be in shock. Did that just happen or was that a dream? I am *for sure* looking for flags because things like this don't happen. I was ready to see a flag for holding. But then I look at Brandon and that's when I knew it.

I will *never* forget the look on his face—a mixture of disbelief and pure joy. It really happened. And just then, I think Case realizes that it really happened. He starts running around like a mad man. *What's he doing?* And then the replay happened, and it was just as loud as when it actually happened. Case running around like a maniac was the cutest thing ever.

Bethany gets me out of my shock and gives me the biggest hug I've ever had. We won. We actually won. It was epic. It was special. It was *miraculous*.

I don't like to leave my seat until Case leaves the field and goes into the tunnel. The crowds die down by then and it's easier to head to the family waiting room. I always have my phone in hand and ignore any text unless it's from Case. He usually gets in touch with me once he gets to the locker room. Sometimes it's quick and sometimes it takes a while, but I have my phone in hand ready to hear from him.

My mind then shifts to logistics. I have to decide who can come down with me to the locker room. I tell most of our friends to just meet me at the restaurant we had picked out before the game. Everyone is taking pictures and hugging. It's a wonderful feeling, but I just want to see my husband. Case calls quicker than I expected and says, "Hey, come down here. I want to see you." So I booked my way up the stairs to get to the elevator to the locker room area as fast as I possibly could.

I decided that only immediate family should come down with me this particular game. We normally aren't able to see players right after the game—we have to wait for them to shower and then come out. Not this time. Case couldn't wait to see us and I couldn't wait to see him.

Throughout my thirteen years of watching Case play, I've gotten a lot of sweaty hugs, but this was definitely the best one yet.

About the Authors

Case Keenum has traveled one of the most unique paths of any NFL quarterback. Case received only one scholarship offer, from the University of Houston, and went undrafted despite breaking multiple NCAA football passing records. He has overcome every obstacle to become a successful starting quarterback. In 2017, Keenum captured America's imagination by leading the Minnesota Vikings to a 13–3 record and an NFC North title. His game-winning touchdown in the final seconds of their divisional playoff game against the Saints, the "Minneapolis Miracle," made Case part of NFL history.

Keenum holds the all-time college football mark for passing yards (19,217), touchdown passes (155), total touchdowns (178), and completions (1,546). He was Conference USA Freshman of the year in 2007, Conference USA Offensive Player of the Year in 2008, and Conference USA Most Valuable Player in 2009 and 2011. He is one of only two quarterbacks to win the Sammy Baugh Award for the nation's outstanding passer twice (2009 and 2011).

Keenum signed with the Houston Texans as an undrafted free agent in 2012. He has a record of 20–18 as an NFL starter with the Texans, Rams, and Vikings. He posted career-highs in passing yards and touchdowns with Minnesota in 2017 and signed with the Denver Broncos in March 2018.

Andrew Perloff is an on-air personality on the television and radio sports talk program "The Dan Patrick Show" and contributing writer for SportsIllustrated.com. Perloff interviewed Keenum for a *Sports Illustrated* feature in 2013 and has covered him throughout his NFL career. Like many others, Perloff alarmed people around him by yelling very loudly during the "Minneapolis Miracle."